The Journey of an Intercessor

PRAYER

By

Dr. Emma T. Warren

© 2018 Dr. Emma T Warren, Chaplain

Publish By

DRETWC

2260 South Ferdon Blvd 110
Crestview, FL 32536

Ministering to the purpose of generations

ISBN-13: 978-1-7325444-0-6

For Worldwide Distribution
This book is printed in the U. S. A.

To reach us on the Internet:

http://www.thompsonwarrenfoundation.com

TABLE OF CONTENTS

ACKNOWLEDGEMENTS

To my Lord and Savior Jesus Christ, I give thanks and all the praise and Glory above all else without the relationship with you and the wisdom, knowledge and understanding I have of you, I could have never attempted such a task of this status.

I thank all the intercessors, family and friends for their prayers, time and support. Special thanks also go to Zarlee Dillon for her prayers and emotional support, her patients, encouragement and assistance during the preparation of this book.

I would like to especially thank all the people that will teach and learn from this book. It is my prayer that this book will be a blessing to the Holy Spirit that is in you and the contents will help and keep you throughout the joinery of your ministry of prayer. And may God grant you Wisdom, Knowledge, Revelation and Understanding of who He truly is. May you always walk in God's GRACE.

DEDICATED TO THE READERS

"Blessed Lord, who hast cause all Holy Scriptures to be for our learning; Grant that we may in such wise hear them, read them, mark them, learn and inwardly digest them, that by patience and comfort of the Holy Word, we may embrace, and ever hold fast, the blessed hope of everlasting life, which is given to us in our Savior Jesus Christ. For it is the Spirit that quickened; the flesh profited nothing: the words that I speak unto you, they are Spirit and they are life."

As the power of our God goes into motion it begins through the confession of God's promises for whatever situation, circumstance, or need you have. As we begin to confess God's Word, a very powerful spiritual principle goes to work in the lives of those who are hearing, reading and reaping the benefit of it.

The Author would like to give thanks to all who read this publication, because, it is dedicated to you; by the grace of God, it is my prayers that the words of God in this publication will bless you, heal you and make you free moving you forward on your journey with Christ. It is my wish that the God of our salvation grant you wisdom, knowledge, understanding and the revelation of His Word that you may know him for yourself.

And may His Holy Spirit be your teacher and lead you into all truths and walk with you daily, blessings to you all.

PREFACE

The Book is for Men and Women that are called into the ministry of prayer for moving forward.

The purpose for which this Book was written is to teach and train men and women that pray to become the Intercessor's for the families and organization and in the everyday fight in your communities and government.

The calling of God's Intercessor is one of the greatest vocations in ministry. One of the biggest problems in ministry today is there are so many leaders that don't have a prayer foundation or intercessors praying for them. It is my mission for the next generations to build strong leaders with strong prayer foundations.

As Intercessors, prayer is a major principle that brings great wisdom for families in your community. The rich man's wealth is his strong city: the destruction of the poor is their poverty. The most important observation of this is that prayer is your communication with God, who can change all things. The mind is either good or evil. Negatively, the mind may be "hardened, "blinded" corrupt and debased. On the positive side, with prayer we may have minds which are renewed and pure. But the only true and lasting wealth of spiritual riches is God's grace.

The book teaches prayer focus on coming together to become the underground part of families and organizations in our or your community that holds the families and organizations in place. We are the source of support and growth. God is not confined to any part of the universe but is present in all His power at every point in space and every moment in time. God created each person for specific reasons, tasks and purposes. God has equipped each one of us with the perfect combination of talents, skills and abilities required to add all fulfillment to our lives with meaning and purpose in our communities.

In this excellent prayer, Solomon does as we should do in every prayer; he gives glory to God. Fresh experiences of the truth of God's promises call for larger praises. He sues for grace and favor from God.

The experiences we have of God's performing his promises, should encourage us to depend upon them, and to plead them with him; and those who expect further mercies, must be thankful for former mercies. God's promises must be the guide of our desires, and the ground of our hopes and expectations in our prayer.

That thine eyes may be open toward this house night and day, even toward the place of which you have said, my name shall be there: that you may hear unto the prayer *which your servant shall make toward this place 1 king 8:29.*

May the Father look upon us in and through his anointed; and may he remember and bless us in all things, according to his mercy to sinners, in and through Christ.

Have respected therefore to the prayer of thy servant, and to his supplication, O LORD my God, to hearken unto the cry and the prayer which your servant prays before thee: (2 Chronicles 6:19)

This also Christ has taught us in his perfect pattern and form of prayer, where there is but one prayer for outward, and all the rest are for spiritual blessings.

The Journey of an Intercessor

The Foundation

The Ultimate Guide to Spiritual Knowledge in the 21st Century

By

DR. EMMA T. WARREN

© JULY 2018

Chapter 1

Prayer

God wants to reveal Himself to every believer: He longs for all believers to know Him, to know Him personally and communicating with God through prayer is how you get to know God personally. The most meaningful prayer comes from a heart that places its trust in the God who has acted and spoken in the Jesus of History and the teachings of the Bible. God speak to us through the Bible, and we in turn speak to Him in trustful, believing prayer.

Effective prayer: The true mark of effective prayer is being a scripturally informed response of person save by grace to the living God who can hear and answer on the basis of Christ's payment of the penalty which sinners deserved. As such, Prayer involves several important aspects such as:

You must master using the word of God or the scriptures in prayer why? Because God's words do not return to him void. The word is your weapon in prayer and is the maine part of your prayer being effective. Let's look at what God has to say about his word:

For my thoughts are not your thoughts, neither are your ways my ways, said the LORD. For as the heavens are higher than the earth, so are my ways higher than your ways, and my thoughts than your thoughts.

For as the rain cometh down, and the snow from heaven, and returned not to that place, but watered the earth, and makes it bring forth and bud, that it may give seed to the sower, and bread to the eater: so, shall my word be that go forth out of my mouth: it shall not return unto me void, but it shall accomplish that which I please, and it shall prosper in the thing whereto I sent it.   Isaiah 55:8-11

In scripture the bible teacher there are many kinds of prayer and an intercessor from time to time use them all. Everyone wants their prayers answered and the different kind of prayers are sure ways for them to be answered.

The Congregation Prayer: Matthew 6:9-13 The Lord Prayer covers everything and when you are in the lowland between ranges of hills or mountains on your journey you will need Psalm 23 to carry you through the valley.

The Closet Prayer: Matthew 6:6 But thou, when you pray, enter into your closet, and when you have shut thy door, pray to thy Father which is in secret; and thy Father which see in secret shall reward thee openly.

The Prayer of Agreement: Mat 18:19 Again I say unto you, that if two of you shall agree on earth as touching anything that they shall ask, it shall be done for them of my Father which is in heaven.

The Prayer of Faith: James 5:15 and the prayer of faith shall save the sick, and the Lord shall raise him up; and if he has committed sins, they shall be forgiven him

The Prayer of Confession: James 5:16 confess your faults one to another, and pray one for another, that ye may be healed. The effectual fervent prayer of a righteous man availed much.

The Prayer of Belief: Matthew 21:22 and all things, whatsoever you shall ask in prayer, believing, you shall receive.

Faith: Having the Belief in or confident attitude toward God, involving commitment to God's will for our life. (Hebrews 11:1-11 17-24 27-31) In the New Testament "faith" covers various levels of personal of commitment.

For which cause, I also suffer these things: nevertheless, I am not ashamed: for I know whom I have believed and am persuaded that he is able to keep that which I have committed unto him against that day.

2 Timothy 1:12

Faith is part of the Christian life from the beginning to end. Faith is the instrument by which we received salvation. The apostle Paul declared that salvation is through faith, not through keeping the works of the law.

For by grace are you saved through faith; and that not of yourselves: it is the gift of God: Not of works, lest any man should boast.

Ephesians 2:8-9

Finally, in the New Testament, faith can refer to the teachings of the bible, the faith which was once for all delivered to the saint (Jude 3). In modern times, faith has been weakened in meaning so that some people use it as self–confidence. But in the Bible, the true faith is confidence in God or Christ not in oneself.

Because we walk by faith and not by sight. 2 Corinthians 5:7 That your faith should not stand in the wisdom of men, but in the power of God (1 Corinthians 2:5) but without faith it is impossible to please him: for those that cometh to God must believe that he is, and that he is a rewarder of them that diligently seek him. (Hebrews 11:6)

Nehemiah's first application was to God, that he might have the fuller confidence in his application to the king. Our best pleas in prayer are taken from the promise of God, the word on which he has caused us to hope. Other means must be used, but the effectual fervent prayer of a righteous man avails most.

Communion with God will best prepare us for our dealings with men. When we have in trusted our concerns to God, the mind is set at liberty; it feels satisfaction and composure, and difficulties vanish. We know that if the affair be hurtful, he can easily hinder it; and if it be good for us, he can as easily forward it.

Let thine ear now be attentive, and thine eyes open, that you may hear the prayer of your servant, which I pray before you now, day and night, for the children of Israel your servants, and confess the sins of the children of Israel, which we have sinned against thee: both I and my father's house have sinned. (Neh1:6)

Our best pleas in prayer are taken from the promise of God, the word on which he has caused us to hope. Other means must be used, but the effectual fervent prayer of a righteous man avails most.

Communion with God will best prepare us for our dealings with men. When we have in trusted our concerns to God, the mind is set at liberty; it feels satisfaction and composure, and difficulties vanish. We know that if the affair be hurtful, he can easily hinder it; and if it be good for us, he can as easily forward it.

Effectiveness in Prayer

Because God is personal, all people can offer prayers. However, sinners who have not trusted Jesus Christ for their salvation remain alienated from God. So, while unbelievers may pray, they do not have the basis for a rewarding fellowship with God. They have not met the conditions laid down in the Bible for effectiveness in prayer. Believers recognize their dependence upon their Creator. They have every reason to express gratitude for God's blessings. But they have far more reason to respond to God than this. They respond to the love of God for them. God's love is revealed through the marvelous incarnation and life of Christ, His atoning provision at the Cross, his resurrection, as well as His continuing presence through the Holy Spirit.

Prayer cannot be replaced by devout good works in a needy world. Important as service to others is, at times we must turn away from it to God, who is distinct from all things and over all things. Neither should prayer be thought of as a mystical experience in which people lose their identity in the infinite reality. Effective prayer must be a scripturally informed response of persons saved by grace to the living God who can hear and answer on the basis of Christ's payment of the penalty which sinners deserved.

The spirit is then most humble, and the heart is broken and tender. It is necessary to exercise faith and hope under afflictions; and prayer is the appointed means for obtaining and increasing these graces. Observe that the saving of the sick is not ascribed to the anointing with oil, but to prayer. In a time of sickness, it is not cold and formal prayer that is effectual, but the prayer of faith.

The great thing we should beg of God for ourselves and others in the time of sickness is the pardon of sin. Let nothing be done to encourage any to delay, under the mistaken fancy that a confession, a prayer, a minister's absolution and exhortation, or the sacrament, will set all right at last, where the duties of a godly life have been disregarded. To acknowledge our faults to each other, will tend greatly to peace and brotherly love. And when a righteous person, a true believer, justified in Christ, and by his grace walking before God in holy obedience, presents an effectual fervent prayer, wrought in his heart by the power of the Holy Spirit, raising holy affections and believing expectations and so leading earnestly to plead the promises of God at his mercy-seat, it avails much.

The power of prayer is proved from the history of Elijah. In prayer we must not look to the merit of man, but to the grace of God. It is not enough to say a prayer, but we must pray in prayer. Thoughts must be fixed, desires must be firm and ardent, and graces exercised. This instance of the power of prayer encourages every Christian to be earnest in prayer. God never says to any of the seed of Jacob, Seek my face in vain. Where there may not be so much of miracle in God's answering our prayers, yet there may be as much of grace.

In every prayer we must make confession, not only of the sins we have been guilty of, but of our faith in God, and dependence upon him, our sorrow for sin, and our resolutions against it. It must be our confession, the language of our convictions. Here is Daniel's humble, serious, devout address to God; in which he gives glory to him as a God to be feared, and as a God to be trusted.

We should, in prayer, look both at God's greatness and his goodness, his majesty and mercy. Here is a penitent confession of sin, the cause of the troubles the people for so many years groaned under. All who would find mercy must thus confess their sins.

Here is a self-abasing acknowledgment of the righteousness of God; and it is evermore the way of true penitents to justify God. Afflictions are sent to bring men to turn from their sins, and to understand God's truth. Here is a believing appeal to the mercy of God. It is a comfort that God has been always ready to pardon sin. It is encouraging to recollect that mercies belong to God, as it is convincing and humbling to recollect that righteousness belongs to him. There are abundant mercies in God, not only forgiveness, but forgiveness's. Here are pleaded the reproach God's people was under, and the ruins God's sanctuary was in. Sin is a reproach to any people, especially to God's people.

The desolations of the sanctuary are grief to all the saints. Here is an earnest request to God to restore the poor captive Jews to their former enjoyments. O Lord, hearken and do. Not hearken and speak only but hearken and do; do that for us which none else can do; and defer not. Here are several pleas and arguments to enforce the petitions. Do it for the Lord Christ's sake; Christ is the Lord of all. And for his sake God causes his face to shine upon sinners when they repent and turn to him. In all our prayers this must be our plea, we must make mention of his righteousness, even of his only. The humble, fervent, believing earnestness of this prayer should ever be followed by us.

Daniel learned from the books of the prophets, especially from Jeremiah, that the desolation of Jerusalem would continue seventy years, which were drawing to a close. God's promises are to encourage our prayers, not to make them needless; and when we see the performance of them approaching, we should more earnestly plead them with God.

Whenever we enter into communion with God, it becomes us to have a due sense of the infinite distance between us and the holy God. How shall we, that are dust and ashes, speak to the Lord of glory? Nothing is more likely, nothing more effectual to revive the drooping spirits of the saints, than to be assured of God's love to them. From the very first day we begin to look toward God in a way of duty, he is ready to meet us in the way of mercy.

While Satan and his angels, and evil counselors, excite princes to mischief against the church, we may rejoice that Christ our Prince, and all his mighty angels, act against our enemies; but we ought not to expect many to favor us in this evil world. Yet the whole counsel of God shall be established; and let each one pray, Lord Jesus, be our righteousness now, and you will be our everlasting confidence, through life, in death, at the day of judgment, and for evermore.

And behold, a hand touched me, which set me shaking on my knees and the palms of my hands. And he said to me, O Daniel, a man greatly beloved, understand the words that I speak to you, and stand upright. For to you I am now sent. And when he had spoken this word to me, I stood trembling. Then he said to me, do not fear, Daniel; for from the first day that you set your heart to understand and to chasten yourself before your God, your words were heard.

Now, my God, let, I beseech thee, thine eyes be open, and let thine ears be attend unto the prayer that is made in this place.
2 Chronicles 6:40

May the Father look upon us in and through his Anointed; and may he remember and bless us in all things, according to his mercy to sinners, in and through Christ. And may our hearts become his resting-place; may Christ dwell therein by faith, consecrating us as his temples, and shedding abroad his love in our prayers.

This also we have been taught to us in his perfect pattern and form of prayers, where there is but one prayer for outward, and all the rest are for spiritual blessings. Now therefore arise, O LORD God, into thy resting place, thou, and the ark of thy strength: let thy priests, O LORD God, be clothed with salvation, and let thy saints rejoice in goodness. 2 Chronicles 6:41

The Aspects of Prayer

Prayer is not only response to God's grace as brought to us in the life and work of Jesus and the teaching of Scripture; it is also request for our needs and the needs of others. There are nine (9) important aspects of prayer; Faith, Worship, Confession, Adoration, Thanksgiving Praise, Dedicated Action, Request and Effectiveness.

Faith: the most meaningful prayer comes from a heart that places its trust in the God who has acted and spoken in the Jesus of history and the teaching of the Bible. God speaks to us through the Bible, and we in turn speak to him in trusting, believing prayer. Assured by the Scripture that God is personal, living, active, all-knowing, all-wise, and all powerful, we know that God can hear and help us.

Worship: In worship we recognize what is of highest worth- not ourselves, others, or our work, but God. Only the highest divine being deserves our highest respect. Guided by Scripture, we set our values in accord with God's will and perfect standards. Before God, angles hide their faces and cry, Holy, Holy, and Holy is the Lord of host.

Confession: Awareness of God's holiness leads to consciousness of our own sinfulness. Like the prophet Isaiah, we exclaim, "Woe is me, for I am undone! Because I am a man or woman of unclean lips, and I dwell in the midst of a people of unclean lips; for my eyes have seen the King, the Lord of hosts" (Isa 6.5). By sinning we hurt ourselves and those closest to us; but first of all, and worst of all, sin are against God. We should confess our sins directly to God, who promises to forgive us of all our unrighteousness.

Adoration: God is love, and He has demonstrated His love in the gift of His Son. The greatest desire of God is that we love him with our whole being (Matt. 22:37). Our love should be expressed, as His has been expressed, in both deeds and words. People sometimes find it difficult to say to others and to God, "I love you." But when love for God fills our lives, we will express our love in prayer to the one who is ultimately responsible for all that we are.

Praise: The natural outgrowth of faith, worship, confession, and adoration is praise. We speak well of one whom we highly esteem and love. The one whom we respect and love above all others, naturally receives our highest commendation. We praise Him for His" mighty acts according to His excellent greatness! (Ps. 150:2), and for His righteous judgments" (Ps. 119:164). For God, for His works, and for His words, for His people gives Him sincere praise.

Thanksgiving: Are we unthankful because we think we have not received what we deserve? But if we got what we "deserved," we would be condemned because of our guilt. As sinners, we are not people of God by nature. We have no claim upon His mercy or grace. Nevertheless, He has forgiven our sins, granted us acceptance as His people, and given us His righteous standing and a new heart and life. Ingratitude marks the ungodly (Rom 1:21). Believers, in contrast, live thankfully. God has been at work on our behalf in countless ways. So in everything, even for the discipline that is unpleasant, we give thanks. (Col. 3:17; 1 Thess. 5:18).

Dedicated Action: Christ's example does not require us to withdraw from society, but to render service to the needy in a spirit of prayer. He wept over Jerusalem in compassionate prayer, and then He went into the city to give his life a ransom for many. Authentic prayer will be the source of courage and productivity, as it was for the prophets and apostles.

Request: Until we have properly responded to God and His Word, He cannot entrust us with His powerful resources. Prayer is request to a personal Lord who answers as He knows best. We should not think that we will always have success in obtaining the things for which we ask. In His wisdom, God hears and answers in the way that is best.

Effectiveness: Although some people think that prayer is a waste of time, the Bible declares that "the effective, fervent prayer of the righteous man or woman avails much. (James 5:16). Is prayer effective only in the inner lives of those who pray? No, prayer can make a difference in the lives of others. Biblical writers believed prayer for other could result in greater wisdom and power, inward strength, knowledge of

Christ's love, filling with God's fullness; discernment, approval of what is excellent, filling with the frits of righteousness, knowledge of God's will spiritual understanding a life pleasing to God.

And when a righteous person, a true believer, justified in Christ, and by his grace walking before God in holy obedience, presents an effectual fervent prayer, wrought in his heart by the power of the Holy Spirit, raising holy affections and believing expectations and so leading earnestly to plead the promises of God at his mercy-seat, it avails much.

The power of prayer is proved from the history of Elijah. In prayer we must not look to the merit of man, but to the grace of God. It is not enough to say a prayer, but we must pray in prayer. Thoughts must be fixed, desires must be firm and ardent, and graces exercised. This instance of the power of prayer encourages every intercessor to be earnest in prayer. God never says to any of the seed of Jacob, Seek my face in vain. Where there may not be so much of miracle in God's answering our prayers, yet there may be as much of grace.

In a time of sickness, it is not cold and formal prayer that is effectual, but the prayer of faith. The great thing we should ask of God for ourselves and others in the time of sickness is the pardon of sin. Let nothing be done to encourage any to delay, under the mistaken fancy that a confession, a prayer, a minister's absolution and exhortation, or the sacrament, will set all right at last, where the duties of a godly life have been disregarded. To acknowledge our faults to each other, will tend greatly to peace and brotherly love.

O Lord, I beseech thee, let now thine ear be attentive to the prayer of thy servant, and to the prayer of thy servants, who desire to fear thy name: and prosper, I pray thee, thy servant this day, and grant him mercy in the sight of this man for I was the king's cupbearer.   *Nehemiah 1:11*

Nehemiah was the Persian king's cup-bearer. The word will direct and quicken prayer, for by it the Spirit helps our infirmities in prayer. The careful study of God's word will more and more discover to us our own sinfulness, and the plenteousness of his salvation; yes it calls us to mourn for sin, and to rejoice in him. Every discovery of the truth of God should render us more unwearied in attendance on his sacred word, and on his worship.

When confessing our sins, it is good to notice the mercies of God, that we may be the more humbled and ashamed. Let us frequently do so, that we may be kept humble, thankful, and watchful. Let all remember that pride and obstinacy is sins which ruin the soul. But it is often as hard to persuade the broken-hearted to hope, as formerly it was to bring them to fear. A God ready to pardon! Instead of keeping away from God under a sense of unworthiness, let us come boldly to the throne of grace, that we may obtain mercy, and find grace to help in time of need. He is a God ready to pardon.

Chapter 2

Hindrances to Answer Prayers

This kind of absolute, intencse assurance in missing in the false teacher and in anyone else whose mind is not focused upon "the word of our Lord Jesus Christ and the doctrine.... of godliness" that is, the word of God. For good reasons God's holy and wise purpose does not permit Him to grant every petition just as it is asked. There are several hindrances to answered prayer mentioned in the Bible.

- ❖ Iniquity in the heart
- ❖ Refusal to hear God's laws
- ❖ An estranged heart
- ❖ Sinful separation from God
- ❖ Waywardness
- ❖ Offering unworthy sacrifices
- ❖ Praying to be seen of men
- ❖ Pride in fasting and tithing
- ❖ Lack of faith
- ❖ And doubting or double-mindedness.

<u>Iniquity in the heart:</u> We should declare unto those that fear God, what he has done for our souls, and how he has heard and answered our prayers, inviting them to join us in prayer and praise; this will turn to our mutual comfort, and to the glory of God. We cannot share these spiritual privileges, if we retain the love of sin in our hearts, though we refrain from the gross practice, Sin, regarded in the heart, will spoil the comfort and success of prayer; for the sacrifice of the wicked is an abomination of the Lord.

But if the feeling of sin in the heart causes desires to be rid of it; if it be the presence of one urging a demand we know we must not, cannot comply with, this is an argument of sincerity. And when we pray in simplicity and godly sincerity, our prayers will be answered. This prayer will excite gratitude to God who has not turned away our prayer or his mercy from us. It was not prayer that fetched the deliverance, but his mercy that sent it. That is the foundation of our hopes, the fountain of our comforts; and ought to be the matter of our praises.

<u>Refusal to hear God's law:</u> The sinner at whose prayers God is angry is one who obstinately refuses to obey God's commands. He who turns away his ear from hearing the law, even his prayer is a hateful thing. (Pro 28:9)

<u>An estranged heart:</u> The Bible is a sealed book to every man, learned or unlearned, till he begins to study it with a simple heart and a teachable spirit, that he may learn the truth and the will of God. To worship God, is to approach him. And if the heart be full of his love and fear, out of the abundance of it the mouth will speak; but there are many whose religion is

lip-labor only. When they pretend to be speaking to God, they are thinking of a thousand foolish things. They worship the God of Israel according to their own devices. Numbers are only formal in worship.

And their religion is only to comply with custom, and to serve their own interest. But the wanderings of mind, and defects in devotion, which are the believer's burden, are very different from the withdrawing of the heart from God, so severely blamed. And those who make the religion of Believers no more than pretense, to serve a turn, deceive themselves. And as those that quarrel with God, so those that think to conceal themselves from him, in effect charge him with folly. But all their perverse conduct shall be entirely done away.

Sinful separation from God: If our prayers are not answered, and the salvation we wait for is not beaten into shape over the test for us, it is not because God is weary of hearing prayer, but because we are weary of praying. See here sin in true colors, exceedingly sinful; and see sin in its consequences, exceedingly hurtful, separating from God, and so separating us, not only from all good, but to all evil.

Yet saints feed to their own destruction, on infidel and wicked systems. Nor can their skill or craft, in devising schemes, as the spider weaves its web, deliver or save them. No schemes of self-wrought salvation shall avail those who despise the Redeemer's robe of righteousness. Every man who is destitute of the Spirit of Christ runs swiftly to evil of some sort; but those regardless of Divine truth and justice, are strangers to peace.

<u>Waywardness:</u> The Lord calls the Jews "this people," not "his people." They had forsaken his service; therefore, he would punish them according to their sins. He forbade Jeremiah to plead for them. The false prophets were the most criminal of all. The Lord pronounces condemnation on them; but as the people loved to have it so, they were not to escape judgments. False teachers encourage men to expect peace and salvation, without repentance, faith, conversion, and holiness of life. But those who believe a lie must not plead if for an excuse. They shall feel what they say they will not fear.

<u>Offering up un-worthy sacrifices:</u> Sinners ruin themselves by trying to baffle their convictions. Those who live in careless neglect of holy ordinances, who attend on them without reverence, and go from them under no concern, in effect say, the table of the Lord is contemptible. They despised God's name in what they did. It is evident that these understood not the meaning of the sacrifices, as shadowing forth the unblemished Lamb of God; they grudged the expense, thinking all thrown away which did not turn to their profit

      If we worship God ignorantly, and without understanding, we bring the blind for sacrifice; if we do it carelessly, if we are cold, dull, and dead in it, we bring the sick; if we rest in the bodily exercise, and do not make heart-work of it, we bring the lame; and if we suffer vain thoughts and distractions to lodge within us, we bring the torn. And is not this evil? Is it not a great affront to God, and a great wrong and injury to our own souls? In order to the acceptance of our actions with God, it is not enough to do that which, for the matter of it, is good; but we must do it from a right principle, in a right manner, and for a right end.

Praying to be seen of men it is taken for granted today that all who are Disciples of Christ pray. You may as soon find a living man that does not breathe, as a living believer that does not pray. If prayer less, then graceless. The Scribes and Pharisees were guilty of two great faults in prayer, vain-glory and vain repetitions. "Verily they have their reward;" if in so great a matter as is between us and God, when we are at prayer, we can look to so poor a thing as the praise of men, it is just that it should be all our reward.

Yet there is not a secret, sudden breathing after God, but he observes it. It is called a reward, but it is of grace, not of debt; what merit can there be in begging? If he does not give his people what they ask, it is because he knows they do not need it, and that it is not for their good. So far is God from being wrought upon by the length or words of our prayers, that the most powerful intercessions are those which are made with groaning that cannot be uttered. Let us well study what is shown of the frame of mind in which our prayers should be offered and learn daily from Christ how to pray.

Pride in fasting and tithing: Miserable is the condition of those who come short of the righteousness of this Pharisee, yet he was not accepted; and why not? He went up to the temple to pray but was full of himself and his own goodness; the favor and grace of God he did not think worth asking. Let us beware of presenting proud devotions to the Lord, and of despising others.

The publican's address to God was full of humility, and of repentance for sin, and desire toward God. His prayer was short, but to the purpose; God be merciful to me a sinner. Blessed be God, that we have this short prayer upon record, as an answered prayer; and that we are sure that he who prayed it, went to his house justified; for so shall we be, if we pray it, as he did, through Jesus Christ.

He owned himself a sinner by nature, by practice, guilty before God. He had no dependence but upon the mercy of God; upon that alone he relied. And God's glory is to resist the proud and give grace to the humble. Justification is of God in Christ. Therefore, the self-condemned, and not the self-righteous, are justified before God.

Lack of faith: By faith Abel, being dead, yet he speaks; he left an instructive and speaking example. Enoch was translated, or removed, that he should not see death; God took him into heaven, as Christ will do the saints who shall be alive at his second coming.

We cannot come to God, unless we believe that he is what he has revealed himself to be in the Scripture. Those who would find God must seek him with all their heart. Noah's faith influenced his practice; it moved him to prepare an ark.

His faith condemned the unbelief of others; and his obedience condemned their contempt and rebellion. Good examples either convert sinners or condemn them. This shows you how believers, being warned of God to flee from the wrath to come, are moved with fear, take refuge in Christ, and become heirs of the righteousness of faith.

And doubting or double-mindedness: You ask and receive not, because you ask amiss, that you may spend it upon your lusts. (Jam 4:3) Sinful desires and affections stop prayer, and the working of our desires toward God.

And let us beware that we do not abuse or misuse the mercies received, by the disposition of the heart when prayers are granted when men ask of God prosperity, they often ask with wrong aims and intentions.

If we seek the things of this world, it is just in God to deny them. Unbelieving and cold desires beg denials; and we may be sure that when prayers are rather the language of lusts than of graces, they will return empty. Here is a decided warning to avoid all criminal friendships with this world. Worldly-mindedness is enmity to God. An enemy may be reconciled, but "enmity" never can be reconciled.

A man may have a large portion in things of this life, and yet be kept in the love of God; but he who sets his heart upon the world, which will conform to it rather than lose its friendship, is an enemy to God. So that anyone who resolves at all events to be upon friendly terms with the world must be the enemy of God.

This is the foundation to learn on your journey as you strive to become an Intercessor. Learn it well that you may grow into your next level as an Intercessor.

And remember on your prayer journey you never stop growing and taking off everything that is contrary to the word of God in your life. Strive to be of excellent quality in God and in all that you do.

Hindrances Blocking Answer

<u>How to Alleviate:</u> We should prove our tempers, conduct, and experience, as gold is assayed or proved by the touchstone. Examine your selves, whether you are in the faith; prove your own selves. For if we would judge ourselves, we should not be judged. 1&2 Corinthians 13:5 11:31

<u>Praying Correctly:</u> There is a divine order to praying:

(1) Entering in: Be careful for nothing; but in everything by prayer and supplication with thanksgiving let your requests be made known unto God. In everything give thanks: for this is the will of God in Christ Jesus concerning you. Giving thanks always for all things unto God and the Father in the name of our Lord Jesus Christ; submitting yourselves one to another in the fear of God, and Enter into his gates with thanksgiving, and into his courts with praise: be thankful unto him and bless his name. *Philemon 4:6, 1 Thessalonians 5:18, Ephesians 5:20-21, Psalms 100:4*

(2). First of all, we all must know Jesus because he is the one that sit at the right hand of the Father and make intercession for us all and then comes these scriptures: I exhort therefore, that, first of all, supplications, prayers, intercessions, and giving of thanks, be made for all men; For kings, and for all that are in authority; that we may lead a quiet and peaceable life in all godliness and honesty. For this is good and acceptable in the sight of God our Savior, who will have all men to be saved and to come into the knowledge of the

truth. For there is one God, and one mediator between God and men, the man Christ Jesus;
1st Timothy 2:1-4

(3). Use God's Word: Then said the LORD unto me, thou hast well seen: for I will hasten my word to perform it. So, shall my word be that go forth out of my mouth: it shall not return unto me void, but it shall accomplish that which I please, and it shall prosper in the thing whereto I sent it. Take your words, and turn to the LORD: say unto him, take away all iniquity, and receive us graciously: so, will we render the calves of our lips. He that turns away his ear from hearing the law, even his prayer shall be abomination. If you abide in me, and my words abide in you, you shall ask what you will, and it shall be done unto you. *Jeremiah 1:12, Isaiah 55:11, Hosea 14:2, Proverbs 28:9, John 15:7*

Doubt-Unbelief: Anxiety is opposite of trust and the prayer of doubt negate the prayer of faith, and the prayer of faith shall save the sick, and the Lord shall raise him up; and if he has committed sins, they shall be forgiven him.

And them that believe: He that believeth and is baptized shall be saved; but he that believeth not shall be damned. And these signs shall follow them that believe; in my name shall they cast out devils; they shall speak with new tongues; they shall take up serpents; and if they drink any deadly thing, it shall not hurt them; they shall lay hands on the sick, and they shall recover. In the last day, that great day of the feast, Jesus stood and cried, saying, if any man thirst, let him come unto me, and drink. He that believeth on me, as the scripture hath said, out of his belly shall flow rivers of living water. (But this spoke he of the Spirit, which they that believe on him should receive: for the Holy Ghost was not yet given; because that Jesus was not yet glorified.)

Trust: Trust in the LORD with all thine heart; and lean not unto thine own understanding. In all thy ways acknowledge him, and he shall direct thy paths. Be not wise in thine own eyes: fear the LORD and depart from evil.

The evil heart of unbelief: Seeing therefore it remain that some must enter therein, and they to whom it was first preached entered not in because of unbelief, take heed, brethren lest there be in any of you an evil heart of unbelief, in departing from the living God.

Abraham's belief: And being fully persuaded that, what he had promised, he was able also to perform. And therefore, it was imputed to him for righteousness. And the head of Ephraim is Samaria, and the head of Samaria is Remaliah's son. If you will not believe, surely you shall not be established. And Jesus said unto the centurion, go your way; and as you have believed, so be it done unto you. And his servant was healed in the selfsame hour.

James 5:15, Mark 16:16-18, John 7:37-39, Proverbs 3:5-7, Hebrews 4:6, 3:12, Romans 4:20-21, Isaiah 7:9, Matthew 8:13

Un-forgiveness: Do to bitterness and resentment we must include all. For those of you who harbor a guilt complex, you should bind and loose: And I will give unto thee the keys of the kingdom of heaven: and whatsoever thou shalt bind on earth shall be bound in heaven: and whatsoever thou shalt loose on earth shall be loosed in heaven. Verily I say unto you, what so-ever you shall bind on earth shall be bound in heaven: and whatsoever you shall loose on earth shall be loosed in heaven.

Bring your gift before the altar because sinners think, by justifying themselves, they escape being judged of the Lord. The rejection of sinners is the grief of believers: And Samuel said, Hath the LORD as great delight in burnt offerings and sacrifices, as in obeying the voice of the LORD? Behold, to obey is better than sacrifice, and to hearken than the fat of rams.

Gift before the altar, and there remembers that your brother has charge against you; Leave there your gift before the altar and go your way; first be reconciled to your brother, and then come and offer your gift.

The Brethren: And when you stand praying, forgive, if you have charge against any: that your Father also which is in heaven may forgive you your trespasses. But if you do not forgive, neither will your Father which is in heaven forgive your trespasses. Then came Peter to him, and said, Lord, how often shall my brother sin against me, and I forgive him? Till seven times? Jesus said unto him, I say not unto you, UN-till seven times: but, UN-till seventy times seven.

Cleansing of: Then said Jesus, Father, forgive them; for they know not what they do. And they parted his raiment and cast lots. Who's so ever sins you remit, they are remitted unto them; and who's so ever sins you retain, and they are retained. God forgiveness to us is in proportion to our forgiveness to others and we have health for our forgiveness. To whom you forgive anything, I forgive also: for if I forgave anything, to whom I forgave it, for your sakes forgave I it in the person of Christ; Lest Satan should get an advantage of us: for we are not ignorant of his devices.

Blessed is he whose transgression is forgiven, whose sin is covered. Blessed is the man unto whom the LORD imputed not iniquity, and in whose spirit, there is no guile. When I kept silence, my bones waxed old through my roaring all the day long. For day and night your hand was heavy upon me: my moisture is turned into the drought of summer. I acknowledged my sin unto thee, and mine iniquity have I not hid. I said, I will confess my transgressions unto the LORD; and you forgave the iniquity of my sin.

1st John 1:9, Matthew 16:19, 18:18, Matthew 5: 23-24, Mark 11:25-26, Matthew 21-22, Luke 23:34, John 20:23, 2 Corinthians 2: 10-11, Psalms 32:1-5

Obedience: Let us not who uses our liberty, despise our weak brother or sister as ignorant and superstitious. Let not the conscientious believer find fault with his brother or sister, for God accepted him, without regarding the difference of meats. We are all apt to make our own views the standard of truth, to deem things certain which to others appear doubtful. If you be willing and obedient, you shall eat the good of the land:

The Lord's commandment: And you shalt love the Lord your God with all your heart, and with all your soul, and with all entire mind, and with all your strength: this is the first commandment. And the second is like, namely this, you-shall love your neighbors as your-self. There is none other commandment greater than these. Master, which is the great commandment in the law? Jesus said unto him, you shall love the Lord your God with all thy heart, and with all your soul, and with your entire mind. This is the first and great commandment. And the second is like unto it, you shall love your neighbors as your-self. On these two commandments hang all the law and the prophets.

<u>Idleness:</u> Therefore, to him that knows to do good and do it not, to him it is sin. And let us beware that we do not abuse or misuse the mercies received, by the disposition of the heart when prayers are granted. Here is a decided warning to avoid all criminal friendships with this world. Worldly-mindedness is enmity to God.

<u>Cursed things of Images:</u> But the children of Israel committed a trespass in the accursed thing: for Achan, the son of Carmi, the son of Zabdi, the son of Zerah, of the tribe of Judah, took of the accursed thing: and the anger of the LORD was kindled against the children of Israel. And Joshua sent men from Jericho to Ai, which is beside Bethaven, on the east side of Bethel, and spoke unto them, saying go up and view the country. And the men went up and viewed Ai. And they returned to Joshua, and said unto him, let not all the people go up; but let about two or three thousand men go up and smite Ai; and make not all the people to labor thither; for they are but few.

So there went up thither of the people about three thousand men: and they fled before the men of Ai. And the men of Ai smote of them about thirty and six men: for they chased them from before the gate even unto Shebarim and smote them in the going down: wherefore the hearts of the people melted and became as water. And Joshua rent his clothes and fell to the earth upon his face before the ark of the LORD until the eventide, he and the elders of Israel, and put dust upon their heads. And Joshua said, Alas, O Lord GOD, wherefore hast thou at all brought this people over Jordan, to deliver us into the hand of the Amorites, to destroy us?

Would to God we had been content and dwelt on the other side Jordan! O Lord, what shall I say, when Israel turned their backs before their enemies! For the Canaanites and all the inhabitants of the land shall hear of it, and shall environ us round, and cut off our name from the earth: and what wilt thou do unto thy great name? And the LORD said unto Joshua, get thee up; wherefore lies thou thus upon thy face? Israel hath sinned, and they have also transgressed my covenant which I commanded them: for they have even taken of the accursed thing, and have also stolen, and dissembled also, and they have put it even among their own stuff.

Therefore, the children of Israel could not stand before their enemies, but turned their backs before their enemies, because they were accursed: neither will I be with you any more, except ye destroy the accursed from among you. Up, sanctify the people, and say, sanctify yourselves against tomorrow: for thus said the LORD God of Israel, there is an accursed thing in the midst of thee, O Israel: thou canst not stand before thine enemies, until ye take away the accursed thing from among you.

In the morning therefore ye shall be brought according to your tribes: and it shall be, that the tribe which the LORD taketh shall come according to the families thereof; and the family which the LORD shall take shall come by households; and the household which the LORD shall take shall come man by man. And it shall be, that he that is taken with the accursed thing shall be burnt with fire, he and all that he hath: because he hath transgressed the covenant of the LORD, and because he hath wrought folly in Israel.

So, Joshua rose up early in the morning, and brought Israel by their tribes; and the tribe of Judah was taken: And he brought the family of Judah; and he took the family of the Zarhites: and he brought the family of the Zarhites man by man; and Zabdi was taken: And he brought his household man by man; and Achan, the son of Carmi, the son of Zabdi, the son of Zerah, of the tribe of Judah, was taken. And Joshua said unto Achan, my son, give, I pray thee, glory to the LORD God of Israel, and make confession unto him; and tell me now what thou hast done; hide it not from me. And Achan answered Joshua, and said, Indeed I have sinned against the LORD God of Israel, and thus and thus have I done:

When I saw among the spoils a goodly Babylonish garment, and two hundred shekels of silver, and a wedge of gold of fifty shekels weight, then I coveted them, and took them; and, behold, they are hiding in the earth in the midst of my tent, and the silver under it. So, Joshua sent messengers, and they ran unto the tent; and, behold, it was hiding in his tent, and the silver under it. And they took them out of the midst of the tent, and brought them unto Joshua, and unto all the children of Israel, and laid them out before the LORD. And Joshua, and all Israel with him, took Achan the son of Zerah, and the silver, and the garment, and the wedge of gold, and his sons, and his daughters, and his oxen, and his asses, and his sheep, and his tent, and all that he had: and they brought them unto the valley of Achor. And Joshua said, why hast thou troubled us?

The LORD shall trouble thee this day. And all Israel stoned him with stones, and burned them with fire, after they had stoned them with stones. And they raised over him a great heap of stones unto this day. So, the LORD turned from the fierceness of his anger. Wherefore the name of that place was called, the valley of Achor, unto this day.

The graven images of their gods shall you burn with fire: you shall not desire the silver or gold that is on them, nor take it unto you, lest you be snared therein: for it is an abomination to the LORD thy God. Neither shall you bring an abomination into your house, lest you be a cursed thing like it: but you shall utterly detest it, and you shall utterly abhor it; for it is a cursed thing.

Honoring parents, not in-law domination: Honor your father and your mother, as the LORD your God has commanded you; that your days may be prolonged, and that it may go well with you, in the land which the LORD your God giveth you.

Roman 14:2, Isaiah 1:19, Mark 12:30-31, Matthew 22:36-40, James 4:17, Joshua 7, Deuteronomy 7:25-26, 5:16

Hate: A destructive force (self-pity) vs. LOVE creative force: Let those who love **the** LORD **hate** evil, for he guards the lives of his faithful ones and delivers them from the hand of the wicked. If anyone says, "I love God," and hates his brother, he is a liar; for he who does not love his brother whom he has seen cannot love God whom he has not seen. There are six things that the LORD hates, seven that are an abomination to him: haughty eyes, a lying tongue, and hands that shed innocent blood, a heart that devises wicked plans, feet that make haste to run to evil, a false witness who breathes out lies, and one who sows discord among brothers. Psalm 97:101, John 4:20,Proverbs 6:16-19

Love is patient and kind; love does not envy or boast; it is not arrogant or rude. It does not insist on its own way; it is not irritable or resentful; it does not rejoice at wrongdoing but rejoices with the truth. Love bears all things, believes all things, hopes all things, endures all things. This is the heart of a true intercessor 1 Corinthians 13:4-7

Condemnation: For God sent not his Son into the world to condemn the world; but that the world through him might be saved. There is therefore now no condemnation to them which are **in** Christ Jesus, who walk not after the flesh, but after the Spirit.

Insecurity: Being confident of this very thing, that he which hath begun a good work in you will perform it until the day of Jesus Christ: Casting all your care upon him; for he cares for you.

<u>Results of hate:</u> He that hate dissemble with his lips and lay up deceit within him; When he speaks fair, believe him not: for there are seven abominations in his heart. Whose hatred is covered by deceit, his wickedness shall be shewed before the whole congregation. Whoso dig a pit shall fall therein: and he that rolled a stone, it will return upon him, a lying tongue hates those that are afflicted by it; and a flattering mouth work ruin.

<u>Prejudice:</u> He that said he is in the light, and hate his brother, is in darkness even until now. He that love his brother abide in the light, and there is none occasion of stumbling in him. But he that hate his brother is in darkness, and walk in darkness, and know not whither he go, because that darkness has blinded his eyes. I write unto you, little children, because your sins are forgiven you for his name's sake.

<u>Answer:</u> But none who rightly know the heart of men can wonder at the contempt and enmity of ungodly people against the children of God. We know that we are passed from death to life: we may know it by the evidences of our faith in Christ, of which love to our brethren is one. Whosoever hate his brother is a murderer: and you know that no murderer has eternal life abiding in him. Hereby perceive we the love of God, because he laid down his life for us: and we ought to lay down our lives for the brethren. But whoso has this world's good, and see his brother have need, and shuttled up his bowels of compassion from him, how dwell the love of God in him?

My little children, let us not love in word, neither in tongue; but indeed, and in truth. And hereby we know that we are of the truth and shall assure our hearts before him. For if our heart condemns us, God is greater than our heart, and know all things. Beloved, if our heart condemns us not, then have we confidence toward God. And whatsoever we ask, we receive of him, because we keep his commandments, and do those things that are pleasing in his sight.

John 3:17, Roman 8:1, Philemon 1:6, 1 Peter 5:7, Proverbs 26:24-28, I John 2:9-12, 3:15-22

Un-repented: The disgraceful sin in one's life fasters in the soul! As we know there is a difference between willful acts and weakness! Short-coming and weakness make overcomers. Read the book of Revelation chapters 2 and 3 on this subject.

Separates from God Behold, the LORD'S hand is not shortened, that it cannot save; neither his ear heavy that it cannot hear: But your iniquities have separated between you and your God, and your sins have hidden his face from you, that he will not hear. If I regard iniquity in my heart, the Lord will not hear me:

Five kinds of sin Keep back your servant also from presumptuous sins; let them not have dominion over me: then shall I be upright, and I shall be innocent from the great transgression. (Pride, power, position, pleasure and possession are the five sins).

How sin enters I saw among the spoils a goodly Babylonish garment, and two hundred shekels of silver, and a wedge of gold of fifty shekels weight, then I coveted them, and took them; and, behold, they are hiding in the earth in the midst of my tent, and the silver under it. And when the woman saw that the tree was good for food, and that it was pleasant to the eyes, and a tree to be desired to make one wise, she took of the fruit thereof, and did eat, and gave also unto her husband with her; and he did eat.

Isaiah 59:1-2, Psalms 66:18, 19:12-13, Joshua 7:21, Genesis 3:6

Care of Temple of God Where no fear of God is, no good is to be expected. Evil pursues sinners. God is unchangeable. And though the sentence against evil works be not executed speedily, but it will be executed;

Set aside God does not: For I am the LORD, I change not; therefore, you sons of Jacob are not consumed.

Surfeiting is over-indulgence: And take heed to yourselves, lest at any time your hearts be overcharged with surfeiting, and drunkenness, and cares of this life, and so that day come upon you unawares.

It is our responsibility to care even though God heals: And every man that strives for the mastery is temperate in all things. Now they do it to obtain a corruptible crown but we are incorruptible. I therefore so run, not as uncertainly; so, fight I, not as one that beat the air: But I keep under my body, and bring it into subjection.

Lest that by any means, when I have preached to others, I myself should be a castaway. I beseech you therefore, brethren, by the mercies of God, that you present your bodies a living sacrifice, holy, acceptable unto God, which is your reasonable service. And be not conformed to this world: but be you transformed by the renewing of your mind that you may prove; what is that good and acceptable and perfect will of God; when you sit to eat with a ruler, consider diligently what is before you: And put a knife to your throat, if you be a man given to appetite. Be not desirous of his dainties: for they are deceitful meat. Pro 1:6 to understand a proverb, and the interpretation; the words of the wise, and their dark sayings. The fear of the LORD is the beginning of knowledge: but fools despise wisdom and instruction. My son, hears the instruction of thy father, and forsakes not the law of thy mother:

Malachi 3:6, Luke 21:34, 1Corinthians 9:25-27, Romans 12:1-2, Proverbs 23:1-3, 6-8

<u>*Touching God's anointed His Servants*</u>: And God hath set some in the church, first apostles, secondarily prophets, thirdly teachers after; that miracles then gifts of healings, helps, governments, diversities of tongues. And he gave some, apostles; and some, prophets; and some, evangelists; and some, pastors and teachers. Saying Touch not mine anointed and do my prophets no harm (NT). Saying, Touch not mine anointed, and do my prophets no harm. (OT)

And David arose, and came to the place where Saul had pitched: and David beheld the place where Saul lay, and Abner the son of Ner, the captain of his host: and Saul lay in the trench, and the people pitched round about him. Then answered David and said to Ahimelech the Hittite, and to Abishai the son of Zeruiah, brother to Joab, saying, who will go down with me to Saul to the camp? And Abishai said, I will go down with thee. So, David and Abishai came to the people by night: and, behold, Saul lay sleeping within the trench, and his spear stuck in the ground at his bolster: but Abner and the people lay round about him. Then said Abishai to David, God hath delivered thine enemy into thine hand this day: now therefore let me smite him, I pray thee, with the spear even to the earth at once, and I will not smite him the second time. And David said to Abishai, destroy him not: for who can stretch forth his hand against the LORD'S anointed, and be guiltless?

LORD shall smite him; or his day shall come to die; or he shall descend into battle and perish. The LORD for-bid that I should stretch forth mine hand against the LORD'S anointed: but, I pray thee, take thou now the spear that is at his bolster, and the cruse of water, and let us go.

And we beseech you, brethren, to know them which labor among you, and are over you in the Lord, and admonish you; And to esteem them very highly in love for their work's sake. And be at peace among yourselves. For God is not unrighteous to forget your work and labor of love, which ye have shewed toward his name, in that ye have ministered to the saints, and do minister.

1 Corinthians 12:28, Ephesians 4:11, Psalms 105:15, 1 Chronicles 16:22, 1 Samuel 26:5-11, 1 Thessalonians 5:1213 Hebrews 6:10

Fear: The effects of fear cancels prayer and the Fear of the LORD is not the fear of man. Hearken unto me, you that know righteousness, the people in whose heart is my law; fear you not the reproach of men, neither be you afraid of their reviling's. The fear of the LORD is the beginning of wisdom: a good understanding has all they that do his commandments: his praise endures forever.

The fear of man brings a snare: but whoso put his trust in the LORD shall be safe. My son, if thou wilt receive my words, and hide my commandments with thee; So that thou incline thine ear unto wisdom, and apply thine heart to understanding; Yea, if thou cry after knowledge, and lifts up thy voice for understanding; If you seek her as silver, and searches for her as for hid treasures; Then shalt thou understand the fear of the LORD and find the knowledge of God. In God I will praise his word, in God I have put my trust; I will not fear what flesh can do unto me. In God have I put my trust I will not be afraid what man can do unto me.

Then they that feared the LORD spoke often one to another: and the LORD hearkened, and heard it, and a book of remembrance was written before him for them that feared the LORD, and that thought upon his name. And they shall be mine, said the LORD of hosts, in that day when I make up my jewels; and I will spare them, as a man spares his own son that serves him. Then shall you return, and discern between the righteous and the wicked, between him that serve God and him that serve him not.

Natural fear is the body protecting self: religious fear Wherefore the Lord said, forasmuch as this people draw near me with their mouth, and with their lips do honor me, but have removed their heart far from me, and their fear toward me is taught by the precept of men: Therefore, behold, I will proceed to do a marvelous work among this people, even a marvelous work and a wonder: for the wisdom of their wise men shall perish, and the understanding of their prudent men shall be hiding.

Demonic fear-enslaves and torments: For God hath not given us the spirit of fear; but of power, and of love, and of a sound mind. There is no fear in love; but perfect love casted out fear: because fear hath torment. He that fear is not made perfect in love. The unknown terror when you are told you have a deadly sickness takeaway the flow of God's love for healing. But we overcome by the blood of Jesus and the words of our confession reverses the body processes. And they overcame him by the blood of the Lamb and by the word of their testimony; and they loved not their lives unto the death.

Isaiah 51:7,12, Psalms 111:10, Proverbs 29:25, 2:1-5, 56:4,11, Malachi 3:16-18, 4:2, Isaiah 29:13-14, 2 Timothy 1:7 1 John 4:18, Revelation 12:11

Robbing God of His Tithes The tithes are holy and instituted by God's hey belong to Him. Will a man rob God? Yet you have robbed me. But you say where-in have we robbed you: in tithes and offerings. You are cursed with a curse: for you have robbed me, even this whole nation. Bring you all the tithes into the storehouse, that there may be meat in mine house, and prove me now herewith, said the LORD of hosts, if I will not open you the windows of heaven, and pour you out a blessing, that there shall not be room enough to receive it. And all the tithe of the land, whether of the seed of the land, or of the fruit of the tree, is the LORD'S: it is holy unto the LORD. And if a man will at all redeem ought of his tithes, he shall add thereto the fifth part thereof. And concerning the tithe of the herd, or of the flock, even of whatsoever pass under the rod, the tenth shall be holy unto the LORD.

Through disobedience it brought the wrath of God: Read Joshua chapter 7: But all the silver, and gold, and vessels of brass and iron, are consecrated unto the LORD: they shall come into the treasury of the LORD.

The Lord honors: But this I say, He which sowed sparingly shall reap also sparingly; and he which sowed bountifully shall reap also bountifully. Every man according as he purposes in his heart, so let him give; not grudgingly, or of necessity: for God loved a cheerful giver. And God is able to make all grace abound toward you; that you, always having all sufficiency in all things, may abound to every good work: (As it is written, He hath dispersed abroad; he hath given to the poor: his righteousness remained forever. Now he that ministered seed to the sower both minister bread for your food, and multiply your seed sown, and increase the fruits of your righteousness;) Give, and it shall be given unto you; good measure, pressed down, and shaken together, and running over, shall men give into your bosom. For with the same measure that ye mete withal it shall be measured to you again.

This is how God cares for His servants: Distributing to the necessity of saints; given to hospitality. Do you not know that they which minister about holy things live of the things of the temple? and they which wait at the altar are partakers with the altar? And the LORD spoke unto Moses, saying, this is it that belong unto the Levites: from twenty and five years old and upward they shall go in to wait upon the service of the tabernacle of the congregation: And from the age of fifty years they shall cease waiting upon the service thereof, and shall serve no more: But shall minister with their brethren in the tabernacle of the congregation, to keep the charge, and shall do no service. Thus, shalt thou do unto the Levites touching their charge.

Malachi 3:8-10, Leviticus 27:30-32, Joshua 7: 6:19, 2 Corinthians 9:6-10, Proverbs 3:9-10, Luke 6:38, Romans 12:13, 1 Corinthians 9:13, Numbers 8:23-26

<u>*Before Communion Examining You*</u>: This is the subtlest sin, causes disease and unhappiness more than anything in the church: Speak no evil one of another, brethren. He that speaks evil of his brother, and judges his brother, speaks evil of the law, and judge the law: but if you judge the law, you are not a doer of the law, but a judge.

<u>Let us not</u>: Let us not be desirous of vain glory, provoking one another, envying one another.

<u>But let us</u>: And let us consider one another to provoke unto love and to good works.

When criticizing one another in Christ we are not discerning the Lord's body, the church. Wherefore whosoever shall eat this bread, and drink this cup of the Lord, unworthily, shall be guilty of the body and blood of the Lord. But let a man examine himself, and so let him eat of that bread, and drink of that cup. For he that eat and drink unworthily, eat and drink damnation to himself, not discerning the Lord's body.

For this because many are weak and sickly among you, and many sleeps. For if we would judge ourselves, we should not be judged. Let no corrupt communication proceed out of your mouth, but that which is good to the use of edifying, that it may minister grace unto the hearers. And grieve not the holy Spirit of God, whereby you are sealed unto the day of redemption. Let all bitterness, and wrath, and anger, and clam our, and evil speaking, be put away from you, with all malice: And be your kind one to another, tenderhearted, forgiving one another, even as God for Christ's sake hath forgiven you.

1 Corinthians 11:27-31, Ephesians 4:29-32, James 4:11, Romans 15:1-7, Galatians 5:26, Hebrews 10:2

Kind of Faith: Faith comes by hearing the Word of God Roman 10:17 So then faith cometh by hearing, and hearing by the word of God.

The way Jesus equates faith: And when Jesus departed thence, two blind men followed him, crying, and saying, you Son of David, have mercy on us. And when he was come into the house, the blind men came to him: and Jesus said unto them, believe you that I am able to do this? They said unto him, Yea, Lord. Then touched he their eyes, saying, according to your faith be it unto you.

And a certain woman, which had an issue of blood twelve years, and had suffered many things of many physicians, and had spent all that she had, and was nothing bettered, but rather grew worse, when she had heard of Jesus, came in the press behind, and touched his garment. For she said, If I may touch but his clothes, I shall be whole. And straightway the fountain of her blood was dried up; and she felt in her body that she was healed of that plague.

And Jesus, immediately knowing in himself that virtue had gone out of him, turned him about in the press, and said, who touched my clothes? And his disciples said unto him, you see the multitude thronging you, and say you who touched me? And he looked round about to see her that had done this thing. But the woman fearing and trembling, knowing what was done in her, came and fell down before him, and told him all the truth. And he said unto her, Daughter, thy faith hath made you whole; go in peace and be whole of thy plague.

Hold fast: And blessed is she that believed: for there shall be a performance of those things which were told her from the Lord. And being fully persuaded that, what he had promised, he was able also to perform. Let us hold fast the profession of our faith without wavering; (for he is faithful that promised)

Sacrifice for Jesus' prayer of His commitment: And being in an agony he prayed more earnestly: and his sweat was as it were great drops of blood falling down to the ground. And he said, Abba, Father, all things are possible unto thee; take away this cup from me: nevertheless, not what I will, but what thou wilt. "If it be your will"- never said in the bible in relation to a healing or answer prayer, only in prayer of consecration or commitment.

Romans 10:17, Matthew 9:27-29, Marl 5:25-34 Luke 1:45, Romans 4:21, Hebrews 10:23, Luke 22:42, Mark 14:36

Taken away from evil to come: The righteous perish and no man lay it to heart: and merciful men are taken away, none considering that the righteous is taken away from the evil to come. He shall enter into peace: they shall rest in their beds, each one walking in his uprightness.
Isaiah 57:1-2

Time to die: To everything there is a season, and a time to every purpose under the heaven: A time to be born, and a time to die; a time to plant, and a time to pluck up that which is planted; A time to kill, and a time to heal; a time to break down, and a time to build up; A time to weep, and a time to laugh; a time to mourn, and a time to dance; A time to cast away stones, and a time to gather stones together; a time to embrace, and a time to refrain from embracing, A time to get, and a time to lose; a time to keep, and a time to cast away; A time to rend, and a time to sew; a time to keep silence, and a time to speak; A time to love, and a time to hate; a time of war, and a time of peace. What profit hath he that work in that wherein he labors? I have seen the travail, which God hath given to the sons of men to be exercised in it. He hath made everything beautiful in his time: also, he hath set the world in their heart, so that no man can find out the work that God make from the beginning to the end.

I know that there is no good in them, but for a man to rejoice, and to do good in his life. And also, that every man should eat and drink, and enjoy the good of all his labor: it is the gift of God. I know that, whatsoever God doeth, it shall be forever: nothing can be put to it, nor any thing taken from it: and God doeth it, that men should fear before him. That which hath been is now; and that which is to be hath already been; and God require that which is past. And moreover, I saw under the sun the place of judgment, that wickedness was there; and the place of righteousness, that iniquity was there. I said in mine heart, God shall judge the righteous and the wicked: for there is a time there for every purpose and for every work. I said in mine heart concerning the estate of the sons of men that God might manifest them, and that they might see that they themselves are beasts.

For that which befall the sons of men befall beasts; even one thing befalls them: as the one die, so died the other; yet, they have all one breath; so that a man hath no preeminence above a beast: for all is vanity. All go unto one place all are of the dust, and all turn to dust again. Who know the spirit of man that goes upward, and the spirit of the beast that go downward to the earth? Wherefore I perceive that there is nothing better, than that a man should rejoice in his own works; for that is his portion: for who shall bring him to see what shall be after him?

Time allotted for: 3 score and ten years' and as it is appointed unto men once to die but after this the judgment:

Also, with time: For my thoughts are not your thoughts, neither are your ways my ways, said the LORD. For as the heavens are higher than the earth, so are my ways higher than your ways, and my thoughts than your thoughts.

A double portion of God' spirit Elisha had and died of a sickness: And it came to pass, when they were gone over, that Elijah said unto Elisha, ask what I shall do for thee, before I am taken away from you. And Elisha said, I pray you, let a double portion of your spirit be upon me. And he said, you have asked a hard thing: nevertheless, if you see me when I am taken from you, it shall be so unto you; but if not, it shall not be so. When the fruit falls from the tree it is ripe for the picking: so, when it is time to die yield to death: closing earthly healing to the presence of God to a larger life of eternity, when you die in Christ Jesus.

Ecclestasters:3, Hebrews 9:27, Isaiah 55:8-9, 2 Kings 2:9-10

<u>Conditions:</u> Jesus speaking to the multitude and to his disciples the scribes and the Pharisees sit in Moses' seat: All therefore whatsoever they bid you observe, that observe and do; but do not go after their works: for they say, and do not.

For they bind heavy burdens and grievous to be borne: and lay them on men's shoulders; but they themselves will not move them with one of their fingers. But all their works they do for to be seen of men: they make broad their phylacteries and enlarge the borders of their garments; and love the uppermost rooms at feasts, and the chief seats in the synagogues, and greetings in the markets, and to be called of men, Rabbi, Rabbi. But be not you called Rabbi: for one is your Master even Christ; and all you are brethren. And call no man your father upon the earth: for one is your Father, which is in heaven.

Neither be you called masters: for one is your Master, even Christ. But he that is greatest among you shall be your servant. And whosoever shall exalt himself shall be abased; and he that shall humble himself shall be exalted.
Matthew 23:1-12

Chapter 3

Intercession

And He saw that there was no man and wondered that there was no intercessor. Therefore, His own arm brought salvation to Him; and His righteousness sustained Him. (Isa 59:16)

Intercession – the act of petitioning God or praying on behalf of another person or group. The sinful nature of this world separates human beings from God. It has always been necessary, therefore, for righteous individuals to go before God to seek reconciliation between Him and His fallen creation. One of the earliest and best examples of intercession of this type occurs in Genesis 18, where Abraham speaks to God on behalf of Sodom. His plea is compassionate; it is concerned with the well-being of others rather than with his own needs. Such selfless concern is the mark of all true intercession.

But the cause of the Redeemer shall gain a complete victory even on earth, and the believer will be more than conqueror when the Lord receives him to his glory in heaven.

It is generally thought to describe the coming of the Messiah, as the Avenger and Deliverer of his church. There was none to intercede with God to turn away his wrath; none to interpose for the support of justice and truth.

Yet He engaged his own strength and righteousness for his people. God will make his justice upon the enemies of his church and people plainly appear. When the enemy threatens to bear down all without control, then the Spirit of the Lord shall stop him, put him to flight. He that has delivered will still deliver. A far more glorious salvation is promised to be wrought out by the Messiah in the fullness of time, which all the prophets had in view. The Son of God shall come to us to be our Redeemer; the Spirit of God shall come to be our Sanctifier: and the Comforter shall abide with the church forever.

The two who are supposed to have been created angels went toward Sodom. The one who is called Jehovah throughout the chapter, continued with Abraham, and would not hide from him the thing he intended to do. Though God long forbears with sinners, from which they fancy that the Lord does not see and does not regard; yet when the day of his wrath comes, he will look toward them. The Lord will give Abraham an opportunity to intercede with him and shows him the reason of his conduct.

Consider, as a very bright part of Abraham's character and example that he not only prayed with his family, but he was very careful to teach and rule them well. Those who expect family blessings must make conscience of family duty. Abraham did not fill their heads with matters of doubtful dispute; but he taught them to be serious and devout in the worship of God, and to be honest in their dealings with all men. Of how few may such a character be given in our days! How little care is taken by masters of families to ground those under them in the principles of religion! Do we watch from Sunday to Sunday whether they go forward or backward?

Another good example is the intercessory prayers of Moses. The leader of a nation and a righteous man, Moses successfully petitioned God on behalf of the Hebrew people (Ex/ 15:25). Even the Pharaoh asked Moses to intercede for him (EX. 8:28).

But just as righteous men often succeeded in reconciling Creator and creation, the Bible also reminds us that the ongoing sinfulness of people can hinder the effects of intercession (1Sam. 2:25, Jer. 7:16). The sacrifices and prayers of the Old Testament priests ware acts of intercession which point forward the work of Christ. Christ is, of course, the greatest intercessor. He prayed on behalf of Peter (Luke 22:32) and His disciples (John17). Then the most selfless intercession of all, He petitioned God on behalf of these who crucified Him (Luke 23:34). And Jesus said, Father, forgive them, for they do not know what they do. And parting His clothing, they cast lots.

But Christ's intercessory work did not cease when He return to Heaven. In heaven He intercedes for His church. His Holy Spirit pleads on behalf of the individual Christian. Finally, because of their unique relationship to God through Christ, Christians are urged to intercede for all people (1Ti

2:1) First of all, then, I exhort that supplications, prayers, intercessions, and giving of thanks be made for all men. Although Jesus did not use the word integrity, he called for purity of heart, (Mat. 5:8) singleness of purpose (Matt. 6:22) and purity of motive (Matt. 6:1-6).

SPIRITUAL-of the spirit or non-material. The word spiritual refers to non-material things, including a spiritual body (1 Cor. 15:44-46) and spiritual things as distinct from earthly goods (Rom 15:27 1 Cor 9:11). But the most important use of the word is in reference to the Holy Spirit. The Spirit gave the law (Rom 7:14) and supplied Israel with water and food (1 Cor 10:3-4).

The Christian's every blessing is from the Spirit (Eph 1:3) as is his understanding of truth (1 Cor 2:13-15; Col 1:9). His song should be sung in the Spirt (Eph 5:19; Col 3:16), and our ability to understand Scripture correctly is given by the Spirit (Rev 11:8). We are to be so dominated by the Spirit that we can called spiritual. (1 Cor 2:15; Gal 6:1).

SPIRITUAL GIFTS special gifts bestowed by the Holy Spirit upon the Christians for the purpose of building up the church. The list of spiritual gifts in 1 Corinthians 12:8-10 includes wisdom, knowledge, faith, healing, miracles, prophecy, discerning of spirits, speaking in tongues and interpretation of tongues. Similar lists appear in Ephesians 4:7-13 and Romn12:3-8. Since the gifts are of Grace, according to Paul, their use must be controlled by the principle of love-the greatest of all spiritual gifts (1 Corinthians 13). Spirituality in the New Testament a person is spiritual because of the indwelling presence and power of the Holy Spirit and the spiritual gifts which He (the Holy Spirit) imparts to the believer (1 Cor 12:1 Col1:9).

Why You Need the Holy Spirit

"There was a man of the Pharisees, named Nicodemus, a ruler of the Jews: The same came to Jesus by night, and said unto him, Rabbi, we know that you are a teacher come from God: for no man can do these miracles that you do, except God be with him. Jesus answered and said unto him, truly, truly, I say unto you, except a man be born again, he cannot see the kingdom of God. Then Nicodemus said unto him, how can a man be born when he is old? Can he enter the second time into his mother's womb, and be born? Jesus answered truly, truly I say unto you, except a man be-born of water and *of* the spirit, he cannot enter into the kingdom of God. That which is born of the flesh is flesh; and that which is born of the Spirit is spirit. Marvel not that I said unto you, you must be born again."

Our Savior spoke of the necessity and nature of regeneration or the new birth, and at once directed Nicodemus to the source of holiness of the heart. Birth is the beginning of life; to be born again, is to begin to live anew, as those who have lived much amiss, or to little purpose. We must have a, new aims, new principles, new nature and new affections. With our first birth we were corrupt, shape in sin; therefore, we must be made new creatures. No stronger expression could have been chosen to signify a great and most remarkable change of state and character.

We must be entirely different from what we were before, as that which begins to be at any time, is not, and cannot be the same with that which was before. This new birth is from heaven; which was born, not of blood, nor of the will of the flesh, nor of the will of man, but of God and its tendency is to heaven. It is a great change made in the heart of a sinner, by the power of the Holy Spirit. It means that something is done for us, and in us, which we cannot do for ourselves.

The regenerating work of the Holy Spirit is compared to water. It is also probable that Christ had reference to the ordinance of baptism. Not that all those, and those only, that are baptized, are saved; but without that new birth which is wrought by the Spirit, and signified by baptism, none shall be subjects of the kingdom of heaven.

Like-wise the Spirit also helped our infirmities: for we know not what we should pray for as we ought: but the Spirit itself makes intercession for us with groaning's which cannot be uttered. And he that searches the hearts know what the mind of the Spirit is, because he makes intercession for the saints according to the will of God. Roman 8:27

Though the infirmities of Christians are many and great, so that they would be overpowered if left to themselves, yet the Holy Spirit supports them. The Spirit, as an enlightening Spirit, teaches us what to pray for; as a sanctifying Spirit, works and stirs up praying graces; as a comforting Spirit, silences our fears, and helps us over all discouragements. The Holy Spirit is the spring of all desires toward God, which are often more than words can utter. The

Spirit who searches the hearts, can perceive the mind and will of the spirit, the renewed mind, and advocates his cause. The Spirit makes intercession to God, and the enemy prevails not.

But the anointing (Holy Spirit) which you have received of him abide in you, and you need not that any man teaches you: but as the same anointing (Holy Spirit) teaches you of all things, and is truth, and is no lie, and even as it has taught you, you shall abide in him. The Spirit of truth will not lie; and he teaches all things in the present dispensation, all things necessary to our knowledge of God in Christ, and their glory in the gospel.

You need the Holy Spirit because you can't enter the Kingdom of God without the Holy Spirit. We need the Holy Spirit because the Holy Spirit is the one that will not lie and all our Spiritual gifts come from the Holy Spirit. For John truly baptized with water; but you shall be baptized with the Holy Spirit not many days hence. (Acts 1:5) We will have power with the Holy Spirit. We need the Holy Spirit for our prayer language. For he that speak in an unknown tongue speak not unto men, but unto God: for no man understand him; howbeit in the spirit he speaks mysteries.

Wherefore let him that speak in an unknown tongue pray that he may interpret. Get the understanding of this "For if I pray in an unknown tongue, my spirit prays, but my understanding is unfruitful. What is it then? I will pray with the spirit, and I will pray with the understanding also: I will sing with the spirit, and I will sing with the understanding also.

1 Corinthians 14: 2, 13-15

It is enough that He God has engaged to give believers strength equal to their trials and services; that under the influence of the Holy Spirit they may, in one way or other, be witnesses for Christ on earth, while in heaven he manages their concerns with perfect wisdom, truth, and love.

Now we have received, not the spirit of the world, but the spirit which is of God; that we might know the things that are freely given to us of God. Which things also we speak, not in the words which man's wisdom teaches, but which the Holy Spirit teaches; comparing spiritual things with spiritual.

But the natural man receives not the things of the Spirit of God: for they are foolishness unto him: neither can he know them, because they are spiritually discerned.

Wherefore let him that speak in an unknown tongue pray that he may interpret. For if I pray in an unknown tongue, my spirit prays, but my understanding is unfruitful. What is it then? I will pray with the spirit, and I will pray with the understanding also: I will sing with the spirit, and I will sing with the understanding also.
1 Corinthians 14:15

That he would grant you, according to the riches of his glory, to be strengthened with might by his Spirit in the inner man; That Christ may dwell in your hearts by faith; that you, being rooted and grounded in love.

Spirit Fill Prayers

We need the Holy Spirit to operate in spirit filled prayers. So, we may ask the question what are spirit filled prayers? Spirit filled prayers are when you can incorporate Praise, Thanksgiving, Worship and your Spiritual Prayer Language in your prayers as you enter into his gates with thanksgiving, and into his courts with praise: be thankful unto him and bless his name. For the LORD is good; his mercy is everlasting; and know his truth endures to all generations.

Next question, how do I become spirit filled? The Baptism of the Holy Spirit can happen to <u>believers</u> before or after Water Baptism. It can come upon believers while hearing the Word, when the word is coming forth in the power and the anointing of the Holy Spirit and the laying on hands brings receptivity with the manifestation of tongues following. (And when Paul had laid his hands upon them, the Holy Spirit came on them; and they spoke with tongues, and prophesied).

Now you have received, not the spirit of the world, but the spirit which is of God; that you might know the things that are freely given to us of God. Which things also we speak, not in the words which man's wisdom teaches, but which the Holy Spirit teaches; comparing spiritual things with spiritual. But the natural man receives not the things of the Spirit of God: for they are foolishness unto him: neither can he know them, because they are spiritually discerned.

But you, beloved, building up yourselves on your most holy faith, praying in the Holy Spirit, by keeping yourselves in the love of God, looking for the mercy of our Lord Jesus Christ unto eternal life. Jude 1:20-21 Then he answered and spoke to me, saying, this is the word of the LORD to Zerubbabel, saying, not by might, nor by power, but by my spirit, smith the LORD of hosts. Zechariah 4:6

God has revealed true wisdom to us by his Spirit. Here is a proof of the Divine authority of the Holy Scriptures, "For prophecy came not in old time by the will of man: but holy men of God spoke as they were moved by the Holy Spirit. 2Peter 1:21 In proof of the Divinity of the Holy Spirit, observe, that he knows all things, and he searches all things, even the deep things of God. No one can know the things of God, but his Holy Spirit, who is one with the Father and the Son, and who makes known Divine mysteries to his people.

This is most clear testimony, both to the real Godhead and the distinct person of the Holy Spirit. The apostles were not guided by worldly principles. They had the revelation of these things from the Spirit of God, and the saving impression of them from the same Spirit. These things they declared in plain, simple language, taught by the Holy Spirit, totally different from the affected oratory or enticing words of man's wisdom. The natural man, the wise man of the world, receives not the things of the Spirit of God.

The pride of carnal reasoning is really as much opposed to spirituality, as the basest sensuality. The sanctified mind discerns the real beauties of holiness, but the power of discerning and judging about common and natural things is not lost. But the carnal man is a stranger to the principles, and pleasures, and acting's of the Divine life. The spiritual man only, is the person to whom God gives the knowledge of his will. How little have any known of the mind of God by natural power!

Like-wise the Spirit also helped our infirmities: for we know not what we should pray for as we ought: but the Spirit itself makes intercession for us with groaning's which cannot be uttered. And he that searches the hearts know what the mind of the Spirit is, because he makes intercession for the saints according to the will of God.

And the apostles were enabled by his Spirit to make known his mind. In the Holy Scriptures, the mind of Christ, and the mind of God in Christ, is fully made known to us. It is the great privilege of intercessor, that they have the mind of Christ revealed to them by His Spirit. They experience his sanctifying power in their hearts and bring forth good fruits in their lives and in the lives of others." But God hath revealed them to us by his Spirit; for the Spirit searches all things, even the deep things of God (1Corinthians 2:10). Christ by his Spirit dwells in all true believers. Intercessors are holy by profession, and should be pure and clean, both in heart and conversation.

The promises of God are strong reasons for us to follow after holiness; we must cleanse ourselves from all filthiness of flesh and spirit. If we hope in God as our Father, we must seek to be holy as he is holy, and perfect as our Father in heaven. His grace, by the influences of his Spirit, alone can purify, but holiness should be the object of our constant prayers.

If the intercessors of the gospel are thought contemptible, there is danger lest the gospel itself be despised also; and though intercessors must flatter none, yet they must be gentle towards all. Intercessors may not look for esteem and favor, when they can safely appeal to the people, that they have corrupted no man by false doctrines or flattering speeches; that they have defrauded no man; nor sought to promote their own interests so as to hurt any. It was affection to them made the apostle speak so freely to them, and caused him to glory of them, in all places, and upon all occasions.

The apostle desired to preserve the Corinthians from being corrupted by the false apostles. There is but one Jesus, one Spirit, and one gospel, to be preached to them, and received by them, and why should any be prejudiced, by the devices of an adversary, against him who first taught them in faith? They should not listen to men, who, without cause, would draw them away from those who were the means of their conversion.

Blessings were made known to believers, by the Lord's showing to them the mystery of his sovereign will, and the method of redemption and salvation. But these must have been forever hidden from us, if God had not made them known by his written word, preached gospel, and Spirit of truth. Christ united the two differing parties, God and man, in his own person, and satisfied for that wrong which caused the separation.

He wrought, by his Spirit, those graces of faith and love, whereby we are made one with God, and among us. He dispenses all his blessings, according to his good pleasure. His Divine teaching led whom he pleased to see the glory of those truths, which others were left to blaspheme. What gracious promises that is which secures the gift of the Holy Spirit to those who ask him! The sanctifying and comforting influences of the Holy Spirit seal believers and Intercessors as the children and army of God, and heirs of heaven.

These are the first-fruits of holy happiness. For this we were made, and for this we were redeemed; this is the great design of God in all that he has done for us; let all be ascribed unto the praise of his glory.

God has laid up spiritual blessings for us in his Son the Lord Jesus; but requires us to draw them out and fetch them in by prayer as we pray for one another. Even the best intercessor need to be prayed for: and while we hear of the welfare of believers and friends, we should pray for them. Even true believers greatly want heavenly wisdom. Is not the best of us unwilling to come under God's yoke, though there is no other way to find rest for the soul?

Do we not for a little pleasure many times part with our peace? And if we dispute less, and prayed more with and for each other, we should daily see more and more what the hope of our calling is, and the riches of the Divine glory in this inheritance. It is desirable to feel the mighty power of Divine grace, beginning and carrying on the work of faith in our souls. But it is difficult to bring a soul to believe fully in Christ, and to venture its all, and the hope of eternal life, upon his righteousness, nothing less than Almighty power will work this in us in prayer.

Here is signified that it is Christ the Savior, who supplies all the necessities of those who trust in him and gives them all blessings in the richest abundance. And by being partakers of Christ himself, we come to be filled with the fullness of grace and glory in him. How then do those forget themselves who seek for righteousness out of him! This teaches us to come to Christ. And did we know what we are called to, and what we might find in him, surely, we should come and be suitors to him. When feeling our weakness and the power of our enemies, we most perceive the greatness of that mighty power which effects the conversion of the believer and is engaged to perfect his salvation. Surely this will constrain us by love to live to our Redeemer's glory.

Through the person, sacrifice, and mediation of Christ, sinners are allowed to draw near to God as a Father, and are brought with acceptance into his presence, with their worship and services, under the teaching of the Holy Spirit, as one with the Father and the Son. Christ purchased leave for us to come to God; and the Spirit gives a heart to come, and strength to come, and then grace to serve God acceptably.

The apostle charged the Ephesians in the name and by the authority of the Lord Jesus, that having professed the gospel, they should not be as the unconverted Gentiles, who walked in vain fancies and carnal affections. The truth of Christ appears in its beauty and power, when it appears as in Jesus. By the new man, is meant the new nature, the new creature, directed by a new principle, even regenerating grace, enabling a man to lead a new life of righteousness and holiness. This is created or brought forth by God's almighty power. But you shall receive power, after that the Holy Spirit is come upon you: and you shall be witnesses unto me both in Jerusalem, and in all Judaea, and in Samaria, and unto the uttermost part of the earth.

"That you put off concerning the former manner of life **the** old man, which is corrupt according to the deceitful lusts: And be renewed in the Spirit of your mind; And that you put on the new man, which after God is created in righteousness and true holiness. Wherefore putting away lying, speaks every man truth with his neighbor: for we are members one of another. Be angry, and sin not: let not the sun goes down upon your wrath: Neither gives place to the devil. (Ephesians 4:22-27) You can stay the same way you were when you came to Christ, you must change.

Chapter 4

The Authority of the Intercessor

The Keys of Power a phrase used by Jesus to describe the authority given by Him to His disciples. In ancient times a Key expressed the idea of authority, power or privilege. Jesus told Peter that He would give him "the keys of the kingdom of heaven" (Matthew 16:19). The result of this authority in Peter life would be the power to bund or loose. These words for bind and loose stem from Aramaic words which carried the idea of excommunication and reinstatement or determining objects either clean or unclean.

The general Protestant view is that he church is the agent of this power or authority to bind or loose, either through its official leaders or through all believers in the New Testament times when the apostle announced the conditions for entrance into the kingdom. This authority was continued through the preaching of the gospel by Peter and the church as described in the Book of Acts.

And I will give the keys of the kingdom of Heaven to you. And whatever you may bind on earth shall occur, having been bound in Heaven, and whatever you may lose on earth shall occur, having been loosed in Heaven. (Mat 16:19)

Binding and Loosing is a command! The Lord left us these keys to unlock the gates of hell and the authority in His name of Jesus that we may have power over enemy. To bind all the powers of darkness which comes against us and lose all the powers of heaven which are at our disposal, in the name of Jesus. The greater powers are those of God Almighty through His Holy Spirit dwelling in you. Bind evil and loose good.

Disciple: a student, learner, or pupil. In the Bible the word is used most often to refer to a follower of Jesus. The word is rarely used in the Old Testament. Isaiah used the term disciples to refer to those who are taught or instructed. Bind up the testimony; seal the Law among My disciples. (Isa 8:16) The word disciple is sometimes used in a more specific way to indicate the twelve apostles of Jesus. In general, apostles refer to a small, inner group of Jesus' followers; disciples refer to a large group of Jesus' followers, such as the women who stood at Jesus' cross and discovered the empty tomb.

Binding and Loosing: a phrase describing the authority and power that Jesus assigned to His disciples, allowing them to forbid or allow certain kinds of conduct. This phrase occurs only twice in the New Testament, in the first instance (Matt. 16:19). Jesus gave Peter "the keys of the Kingdom of heaven" and told him "whatever you bind on earth will be bound (literally, "shall have been bound") in heaven, and whatever you loose on earth will loosed ("shall have been loosed') in heaven." This means that Peter was granted the authority to pronounce the freedom or condemnation of a person, based on that person's response to the gospel. The tense of the verbs "shall have been" indicates that this fact was already established in the will of the Father. In Matthew 18:18 the same words were spoken by Jesus to all the disciples, granting them authority in matters of church discipline.

Can you imagine how terrible it would be to find yourself a prisoner, locked behind bars where you could not get out! To be bound there in darkness and despair and caged like an animal. To know in your heart, you were created to be free, unshackled to roam the good earth in glorious liberty but, instead the evil enemy captured and robbed you of your freedom. He left you cast down, afflicted, hopeless, and in utter despair!

SUDDENLY! You see a shining light dispelling the darkness, you have a visitor! He appeared as one having all authority; yet, He was gracious and his eyes were full of compassion. He said, "I have a key that open all prison doors." "I came here for this very purpose; to bring deliverance to the captives "to sat free those who are bound by the enemy." To destroy the enemy works." To set at liberty all those who are bound." Can you imagine your reaction? What tender mercy! What underserved grace! To offer Life instead of death! Hope, like a ray of sunshine, springs forth as He inserts those precious keys into the lock. The door swings open! And He says to you "go free". There can be no situation so distressing or dangerous, in which faith will not get comfort from God by prayer.

We are apt to show our troubles too much to ourselves, poring upon them, which does us no service; whereas, by showing them to God, we might cast the cares upon him who care for us, and thereby ease ourselves. Nor should we allow any complaint to ourselves or others, which we cannot make to God. When our spirits are overwhelmed by distress and filled with discouragement; when we see snares laid for us on every side, while we walk in his way, we may reflect with comfort that the Lord know our path.

Those who in sincerity take the Lord for their God find him all-sufficient, as a Refuge, and as a Portion: everything else is a refuge of lies, and a portion of no value. In this situation David prayed earnestly to God. We may apply it spiritually; the souls of believers are often straitened by doubts and fears.

And it is then their duty and interest to beg of God to set them at liberty that they may run the way of his commands. The Lord delivered David from his powerful persecutors and dealt bountifully with him. He raised the crucified Redeemer to the throne of glory and made him Head over all things for his people. The convinced sinner cries for help and is brought to praise the Lord in the company of his redeemed people; and all believers will at length be delivered from this evil world, from sin and death, and praise the Savior forever.

Knowledge: The truth or facts of life that a person acquires either through experience or thought. The greatest truth that a person can possess with the mind or learn through experience is truth about God. Be still and know that I *am* God! I will be praised among the nations; I will be praised in the earth. (Ps 46:10) Come and see the effects of desolating judgments and stand in awe of God. This shows the perfect security of the intercessor and is an assurance of lasting peace. Matthew 6:33 But seek you first the kingdom of God, and his righteousness; and all these things shall be added unto you.

Let us pray for the speedy approach of these glorious days, and in silent submission let us worship and trust in our almighty God. Let all intercessors triumph in this, that the Lord of hosts, the God of Jacob, has been, is, and will be with us; and will be our Refuge. And hath raised us up together and made us sit together in heavenly places in Christ Jesus.

Mark this, take the comfort, and say, If God be for us, who can be against us? With this, through life and in death, let us answer every fear. And you shall know the truth, and the truth shall make you free. They answered Him; we are Abraham's seed and were never in bondage to anyone. How do you say, you will be made free? (John 8:32-33)

Such power and authority attended our Lord's words that many were convinced and professed to believe in him. He encouraged them to attend his teaching, rely on his promises, and obey his commands, notwithstanding all temptations to evil. Behold, I give unto you power to tread on serpents and scorpions, and over all the power of the enemy: and nothing shall by any means hurt you.

In doing, they would be his disciples truly; and by the teaching of his word and Spirit, they would learn where their hope and strength lay. Christ spoke of spiritual liberty; but carnal hearts feel no other grievances than those that molest the body and distress their worldly affairs.

Talk to them of their liberty and property, tell them of waste committed upon their lands, or damage done to their houses, and they understand you very well; but speak of the bondage of sin, captivity to Satan, and liberty by Christ; tell of wrong done to their precious souls, and the hazard of their eternal welfare, then you bring strange things to their ears.

Jesus plainly reminded them, that the man, who practiced any sin, was, in fact, a slave to that sin, which was the case with most of them. Christ in the gospel offers us freedom, he has power to do this, and those whom Christ makes free are really so. But often we see persons disputing about liberty of every kind, while they are slaves to some sinful lust. But where the Spirit of the Lord is, there is liberty.

This cannot be gained by unaided human reason. It is acquired only as God shows Himself to man in nature and conscience in history or providence and especially in the Bible. Mental knowledge by itself, as good as it may be, is inadequate; it is capable only of producing pride.

Casting down imaginations, and every high thing that exalt itself against the knowledge of God and bringing into captivity every thought to the obedience of Christ; And having in a readiness to revenge all disobedience, when your obedience is fulfilled.

Moral knowledge affects a person's will it is knowledge of the heart, not of the mind alone. The Book of Proverbs deals primarily with this kind of knowledge. Experiential knowledge is that gained through one's experience.

"For this cause we also, since the day we heard, do not cease to pray for you, and to desire that you might be filled with the knowledge of His will in all wisdom and spiritual understanding. That you might walk worthy of the Lord to all pleasing, being fruitful in every work and increasing in the knowledge of God, (Col 1:9-10)

The apostle was constant in prayer, that we the believers might be filled with the knowledge of God's will, in all wisdom. Good words will not do without good works. He, who undertakes to give strength to his people, is a God of power, and of glorious power. The blessed Spirit is the author of this. In praying for spiritual strength, we are not straitened, or confined in the promises, and should not be so in our hopes and desires. The grace of God in the hearts of believers and Intercessors is the power of God; and there is His Glory and Authority in this power.

The special use of this strength was for sufferings. There is work to be done, even when we are suffering. Amidst all their trials they gave thanks to the Father of our Lord Jesus, whose special grace fitted them to partake of the inheritance provided for the saints. To bring about this change, those were made willing subjects of Christ, who were slaves of Satan, but now believers of Christ.

Prepare for War

War-Warfare when we use this terminology we know that there is an armed conflict with an opposing military force. Today in America you may say we are looking at a Holy War. From the perspective of the Hebrew people, a holy war was one which God Himself declared, led and won. As you know in our last Presidential election it caused grate conflict with the American people and we are at war with good and evil. Our government has become a posse of evildoers that are workers of iniquity. Generally, the word evildoers are applied to the enemies of God and his people.

America was founded on the principles of God. Now I would say we are in a place like Israel's. The one thing needed for a Holy War is that we are to trust in God without any doubt or reservations because this nation is working on putting it trust in the powers of the day, wealth and political alliances. We are on the road to distraction. The army of God is on its way and you need to prepare for war.

All who are designed for heaven hereafter are prepared for heaven now. Those who have the inheritance of sons, have the education of sons, and the disposition of sons. By faith in Christ they enjoyed this redemption, as the purchase of his atoning blood, whereby forgiveness of sins and all other spiritual blessings were bestowed. Surely then we shall deem it a favor to be delivered from Satan's kingdom and brought into that of Christ, knowing that all trials will soon end, and that every believer will be found among those who come out of great tribulation. Finally, my brethren, be strong in the Lord, and in the power of his might. Put on the whole amour of God that you may be able to stand against the wiles of the devil. For we wrestle not against flesh and blood, but against principalities, against powers, against the rulers of the darkness of this world, against spiritual wickedness in high places.

Wherefore take unto you the whole amour of God that you may be able to withstand in the evil day, and having done all, to stand. Stand therefore, having your loins girt about with truth, and having on the breastplate of righteousness. And your feet shod with the preparation of the gospel of peace; Above all, taking the shield of faith, wherewith you shall be able to quench all the fiery darts of the wicked. And take the helmet of salvation, and the sword of the Spirit, which is the word of God:

Praying always with all prayer and supplication in the Spirit and watching thereunto with all perseverance and supplication for all saints; And for me, that utterance may be given unto me, that I may open my mouth boldly, to make known the mystery of the gospel. Ephesians 6:

Wherefore take unto you the whole amour of God that you may be able to withstand in the evil day, and having done all, to stand. Stand therefore, having your loins girt about with the Holy Spirit of truth, and having on the breastplate of righteousness... now as we sow to ourselves in righteousness, reap in mercy; break up your fallow ground: for it is time to seek the LORD, till he come and rain righteousness upon us. *Hosea 10:12*... no good thing will he withhold from them that walk uprightly... but the desire of the righteous shall be granted. And your feet shod with the preparation of the gospel of peace... And the peace of God, which passes all understanding, shall keep your hearts and minds through Christ Jesus. For he is our peace, who hath made both one, and hath broken down the middle wall of partition between us; Above all, taking the shield of faith... that your faith should not stand in the wisdom of men, but in the power of God. now faith is the substance of things hoped for, the evidence of things not seen. But without faith it is impossible to please him: for he that comes to God must believe that he is, and that he is a rewarder of them that diligently seek him, wherewith you shall be able to quench all the fiery darts of the wicked.

And take the helmet of salvation...That if you shalt confess with your mouth the Lord Jesus, and shalt believe in your heart that God has raised him from the dead, you shalt be saved. For with the heart man believes unto righteousness; and with the mouth confession is made unto salvation. For whosoever shall call upon the name of the Lord shall be saved and the sword of the Spirit which is the word of God... He sent his word, and healed them, and delivered them from their destructions. Order my steps in your word: and let not any iniquity have dominion over me. Your word is a lamp unto my feet, and a light unto my path. It is written, Man shall not live by bread alone, but by every word that proceed out of the mouth of God.

Praying always with all prayer and supplication in the Spirit and watching thereunto with all perseverance and supplication for all saints; And for me, that utterance may be given unto me, that I may open my mouth boldly, to make known the mystery of the gospel. Knowledge is given to the apostles to open spiritual things in scriptures, of revelation knowledge to be revealed by His Anointed to His people. Therefore, our greatest weapons as intercessors for the battle between the enmity of the flesh, the soul, and the spirit; the warfare which goes on in the heart and mind is that all evil can be bound in the name of Jesus. It is our use of powers of God delegated to us in the name of Jesus that overcomes evil with good!

Know this, the most powerful weapon is the word of God, "...His name is called the word of God!" Rev 19: 13b for the word of God is quick, and powerful, and sharper than any two-edged sword, piercing even to the dividing asunder of soul and spirit, and of the joints and marrow, and is a discerner of the thoughts and intents of the heart. The grass withered, the flower faded: because the spirit of the LORD blow upon it: surely the people is grass. The grass withered, the flower fades: but the word of our God shall stand for ever. So, shall my word be that go forth out of my mouth: it shall not return unto me void, but it shall accomplish that which I please, and it shall prosper in the thing whereto I sent it.

His Part and Our Part

These shall war against the Lamb, and the Lamb shall overcome them, for he is Lord of Lords and King of kings; and they also shall overcome that are with him, called and chosen and faithful Rev 17:14

You May be called. You may be chosen. But only the FAITHFUL ones will be at His side when He conquers the enemy! So, remember the calling and choosing is His part. But to be faithful is YOUR part. <u>Faithful:</u> to stand firm, to trust, to be certain, and to believe in God for all things.

The believer's choice to do or not to do…binding and loosing is the believer's choice. What is our part in the action of binding and loosing? The Bible says, you bind and loose. I will give unto thee the keys of the kingdom of heaven: and whatsoever thou bind on earth shall be bound in heaven; and whatsoever thou loose on earth shall be loosed in heaven. (Mat 16:19) Let us examine this power to bind; our part in this work is to decide what needs to be done; to determine if there is fruit of an evil spirit. If so, we must first bind that spirit, then speak destruction to the fruit that is producing.

<u>Next:</u> we must deal with past damages done by these evil ones. Then, to decree it, as a king, to say it either out loud or silently to God, and to believe God's Word is true. After we have finish this work of God, our part of the action ends, and God's part begins. God is the only one that takes chains and ropes and tie up, not you. Verily I say unto you, what things so ever you shall bind on earth shall be bound in heaven; and what things so ever you shall loose on earth shall be loosed in heaven (Mat 18:18) that is God's Word!

Our part is to be faithful. The binder is given authority and power from on High. God binds whatever we bind from operating any place in the heavenly or the earthly realm. In any given situation the believer (Key Holder) have the power to bind. The principles of these rules may be practiced everywhere, and under all circumstances, though they are too much neglected by all. But how few try the method which Christ has expressly given this power to all his disciples (the Believer's and the Intercessors)!

In all our proceedings we should seek direction in prayer; we cannot too highly prize the promises of God. Wherever and whenever we meet in the name of Christ, we should consider him as present in the midst of us. Peter, for himself and his brethren, said that they were assured of our Lord's being the promised Messiah, the Son of the living God. This showed that they believed Jesus to be more than man.

Our Lord declared Peter to be blessed, as the teaching of God made him differ from his unbelieving countrymen. Christ added that he had named him Peter, in allusion to his stability or firmness in professing the truth. The word translated "rock," is not the same word as Peter, but is of a similar meaning. Nothing can be more wrong than to suppose that Christ meant the person of Peter was the rock. Without doubt Christ himself is the Rock, the tried foundation of the believer; and woe to him that attempts to lay any other! Peter's confession is this rock as to doctrine. If Jesus be not the Christ, those that own him are not of the believers, but deceivers and deceived.

Our Lord next declared the authority with which Peter would be invested. He spoke in the name of his brethren, and this related to them as well as to him. They had no certain knowledge of the characters of men and were liable to mistakes and sins in their own conduct; but they were kept from error in stating the way of acceptance and salvation, the rule of obedience, the believer's character and experience, and the final doom of unbelievers and hypocrites. In such matters their decision was right, and it was confirmed in heaven. But all pretensions of any man, either to absolve or retain men's sins, are blasphemous and absurd. None can forgive sins but God only. And this binding and loosing, in the common language of the Jews, signified to forbid and to allow, or to teach what is lawful or unlawful.

God binds to the extent that you spoke it. If you restrict it to a certain area or decide to commit a spirit to a certain place, then that is what He will do. We have been given His Sanction to do as we decide because it is the ability and knowledge to bind and loose that is going to kelp bring in the kingdom of God! The enemy, obstacles, and opposition must be bound and remove in order to get on with the work and business of God.

For instance, Binding and Casting out could be used to relocate opposing spirits so we can be free to come and go at liberty. For example, if we are sent somewhere and cannot get to our destination because of an obstacle placed in our path, say to it, "Be removed and cast into the sea," and it shall be done by our Father. As God's believers we should be the over-comes in all things. We are not to go up to the mountain or obstacle and to God, "I'm sorry, I can't get this job done. An evil spirit withstood me, and I could not do it, so I gave up." No, that excuse will not do.

Make a decision of exactly what you need done to get God's will accomplished. Then SPEAK it to the object before God. (It is not necessary to speak aloud unless led by the Holy Spirit. You are not dealing with flesh and blood, but with principalities and powers of darkness of this world.) God is saying YOU BIND IT, I BIND IT...YOU LOOSE AND I LOOSS." Let's get on with it. We have the power to move things and persons around with the Holy Spirit in order to do the will of the Father. That is the power believers and intercessors have when they are (Filled with the Holy Spirit).

Binding and Loosing makes a real difference in any given situation. To bind an enemy or an evil work, and loose a friend, and a good work, is the mighty Power given to the believer to bring about God's will upon the earth even as it is now in Heaven. We set free the human body from evil powers that cause sickness, sorrow, un-soundness, un-happiness, torment, captivity, etc. We have been given POWER over all the power of evil-why should WE knuckle under?

Let them crumble under Our Authority! Don't let Satan get away with it, God allows what we allow and disallows what we disallow. Do don't allow it, restrict, constrain, confine and yes bind it.

The definition of Binding: To bind, to fasten by a band, chain, or ropes, etc., to tie, make rigid, firm, unmovable, fasten, shackle, fetter, cinch, clamp, manacle, pin, hitch, secure, peg down, strap down, or tether, confine tighten, slow down, close down, stop, or put an end to. *To restrain:* constrain, hinder, put under a pace bound, arrest, restrict, forbid, refuse to allow. ***Always by Authority:*** whether Spiritual authority, governmental authority, or brute force. In our case, it is Spiritual Authority of holding the three keys: Binding, Loosing, and Knowledge.

The Definition of Loosing: To set free, unfasten, unbind, untie, release, separate, remove, relocate, lift the barriers, pardon, to forgive, to exonerate, to clear or absolve from guilt, to lose form blame, pressures, tensions, torments, domination by others, living or dead, too lose from demons, diseases, and curses. *Some of the things people need to be loosed from:* Devil, demons, evil angles, familiar spirits, evil traits, curses, and inherited diseases. *The living evil:* Witches, sorcerers, mediums, magicians, adepts, false teachers, false prophets and sinners. *Witchcraft:* Psychic heredity, psychic powers, habits, sins, charms, vexes spells, jinxes, and bewitchments. If the devil has bound something or someone so they cannot have liberty-Unbind them and let them go free.

Even the greatest of men may be much in trouble. Neither the crown on the king's head, nor the grace in his heart, would make him free from trouble. Even the greatest of men must be much in prayer. Let none expect benefit by the prayers of the believers and intercessors, or their friends, who are capable of praying for them, yet neglect it. Pray that God would protect his person and preserve his life. That God would enable him to go on in his undertakings for the public good.

We may know that God accepts our spiritual sacrifices, if by his Spirit he kindles in our souls a holy fire of piety and love to God; believe that the Lord would crown his enterprises with success. Our first step to victory in spiritual warfare is to trust only in the mercy and grace of God; all who trust in themselves will soon be cast down. Believers and intercessors triumph in God, and his revelation of himself to them, by which they distinguish themselves from those that live without God in the world.

Though men are false, God is faithful; though they are not to be trusted, God is. The preciousness of God's word is compared to silver refined to the highest degree. How many proofs have been given of its power and truth! God will secure his chosen remnant however bad the times are.

As long as the world stands, there will be a generation of proud and wicked men. But all God's people are put into the hands of Christ our Savior; there they are in safety, for none can pluck them out of God's hand; being built on Him, the Rock, they are safe, notwithstanding temptation or persecution come with ever so much force upon them. To meditate in God's word, is to discourse with ourselves concerning the great things contained in it, with close application of mind and fixedness of thought. We must have constant regard to the word of God, as the rule of our actions, and the spring of our comforts; and have it in our thoughts night and day. For this purpose, no time is amiss.

These enemies can show no good cause for opposing so just and holy a government, which, if received by all, would bring a heaven upon earth. They can hope for no success in so opposing so powerful a kingdom of our Lord and Savior Jesus Christ. The Lord Jesus has all power both in heaven and in earth and is Head over all things to the believers and intercessors, notwithstanding the restless endeavors of his enemies. Christ's throne is set up in his believes and intercessors, that is, in the hearts of all believers and intercessors.

Chapter 5

The Duties of Intercessors

Praying always with all prayer and supplication in the Spirit and watching thereunto with all perseverance and supplication for all saints; And these signs shall follow them that believe; in my name shall they cast out devils; they shall speak with new tongues; they shall take up serpents; and if they drink any deadly thing, it shall not hurt them; they shall lay hands on the sick, and they shall recover. Ephesians 6:18 Mark 16:15-18

We believe the following is the list of the duties that are be expected as an Intercessor. The list does not include all the responsibilities that an Intercessor can undertake, but this is a good place to start.

It is Your Duty to Pray in Boldness

Let us therefore come boldly unto the throne of grace that we may obtain mercy and find grace to help in time of need. Settle it therefore in your hearts, not to meditate before what you shall answer: For God will give you a mouth and wisdom, which all your adversaries shall not be able to gainsay nor resist according to the eternal purpose which he purposed in Christ Jesus our Lord: In whom we have boldness and access with confidence by the faith of him.

Hebrews 4:16 Luke 21:14-15 Ephesians 3:12

Your Duty to Know God's Word

Jesus answered and said unto them, you do err, not knowing the scriptures, or the power of God. For God is not a man that he should lie neither the son of man that he should repent: hath he said, and shall he not do it? Or hath he spoken, and shall he not make it good? To the Intercessor God's word are a lamp unto your feet, and a light unto my path.

Matthew 22:29 Numbers 23:19 Psalms 119:105

Your Duty to Pray for Wisdom

For the LORD giveth wisdom: and out of his mouth come knowledge and understanding. He lay up sound wisdom for the righteous: he is a buckler to them that walk uprightly. If you don't have wisdom If any of you lack wisdom, let him ask of God, that giveth to all men liberally, and upbraided not; and it shall be given him. But the Comforter, which is the Holy Ghost, whom the Father will send in my name, he shall teach you all things, and bring all things to your remembrance, whatsoever I have said unto you. But the anointing which ye have received of him abided in you, and ye need not that any man teaches you: but as the same anointing teaches you of all things, and is truth, and is no lie, and even as it hath taught you, ye shall abide in him.

Proverbs 2:6-7 James 1:5 John 14:26 1John 2:27

Your Duty to Pray with Confidence

And this is the confidence that we have in him that, if we ask any thing according to his will, he hears us: And if we know that he hear us, whatsoever we ask, we know that we have the petitions that we desired of him. For thus said the Lord GOD, the Holy One of Israel; in returning and rest shall you be saved; in quietness and in confidence shall be your strength. Be still and know that I am God: I will be exalted among the heathen; I will be exalted in the earth. For we are made partakers of Christ if we hold the beginning of our confidence steadfast unto the end!

1John 5:14-15 Isa 30:15 Psalms 46:10 Hebrews3:14

Your Duty Not to Be Wicked

Let the wicked forsake his way, and the unrighteous man his thoughts: and let him return unto the LORD, and he will have mercy upon him; and to our God, for he will abundantly pardon. Search me, O God, and know my heart: try me, and know my thoughts: And see if there be any wicked way in me and lead me in the way everlasting.

Isaiah 55:7 Psalms 139:23-24

The Intercessors Ministry

Under spiritual guidance there are two important functions of the intercessor they are to pray for individuals and their families in times of crises or in emergency and to help them with their spiritual needs in prayer. Of all the many duties the Intercessor may entail, these are the principal responsibilities they have.

The intercessors may use different ways to bring about spiritual truths and assistance to an individual or family. However, the most important ministry is to simply be available when called upon. Spiritual need is the greatest of all needs and the Intercessor must be able to meet this need. The Intercessor ministry is a ministry of action rather than word.

The ministry of Intercessor's to me is the greatest Ministry of all. Why? Because intercessors are always in God's present and it has always been necessary, therefore, for righteous individuals to go before God in prayer to seek reconciliation between Him and His fallen creation. People come to Christ for salvation because there is an intercessor some ware laboring in praying for their salvation.

In my ministry of intercession God shiftiest our prayers to praying for child abuse children because it had gotten so bad that every time you turn on the TV there was some kind of child abuse and there was no one praying for them. After we started praying for the children God started making provision by using churches to build and open up safe places for them go. People that are lost and have no hope God's chosen intercessors are praying on their behalf.

Assistance in Emergency Situations

Another important part of these functions is to understand the personal spiritual needs of the individual and to call their own Chaplain or Minister to assist as soon as possible, if the family so desires. The intercessor can then assist their Chaplain or Minister to understand the functions and the resources available through the Ministry.

At or in emergency incidents you as an Intercessor, if not involved in the actual work of the emergency, should be alert to the needs of the emergency service holding them up in prayer. The Intercessor should be especially mindful that the type of people making emergency response is easily capable of overexerting themselves to the point that they could drive themselves to exhaustion that is why you as an intercessor should be holding them up in prayer.

The importance of keeping a cool, calm demeanor during these times you along with the ability to plead for their need by interceding for them is a service you the Intercessor can perform. Find you a quite spot or closet and began to interceding because when you pray, you enter into your closet, and when you shut the door, pray to your Father which is in secret; and your Father who see you in secret shall reward you openly.

But thou, when thou pray, enter into thy closet, and when thou hast shut thy door, pray to thy Father which is in secret; and thy Father which see in secret shall reward thee openly.
Matthew 6:6

Comforting the situations in prayer and offering positive direction to the victim family in prayer will be priorities at these types of incidents. Intercessors that act in these ways at the site of an emergency, the results are generally successful in not only aiding the victims but also helping to move the Father to action.

Intercessors with Hospitals and Clinics

An Intercessor should frequently visit hospitals and clinics in the widest sense of the words, to build prayer rapport with medical personnel or just walk the halls and quietly pray.

These visits help the Intercessor to receive accurate and helpful reports from the hospital professionals who have confidence in the Intercessor with whom they have become acquainted or the Holy Spirit will give you what to pray for.

In not breaking any laws this information helps intercessors to help the families in prayer when they understanding what is taking place and to better understand how to pray for the condition of their patient. God will put you in situations that will become your training ground, He did it to me. My training as an intercessor was how I develop in the most meaningful way was praying.in Hospitals and Clinics.

I had pulmonary issues and if I sat in the room with or ware anyone smoked three days later I was in the Emergency Room. I went so often that the Doctors and Nurses knew me by name. My treatment would some time take two to three hours and I would lay there and read my bible and pray.

One night I was laying in the emergency room getting my treatments and a nurse came to me and told me that it had been a real bad accident and would I pray for the ones that had been in the accident. I said yes, so I laid there in my quite spot and prayed in the Spirit for them. Because I knew the scriptures I prayed in the Spirit.

Likewise, the Spirit also helps our infirmities: for we know not what we should for as we ought: but the Spirit itself make intercession for us with groaning's which cannot be uttered.
Roman 8:26

From that day on when I would go to the emergency room and any of my clinic appointments I would pray for every one there and I no longer just prayed for myself and that is what developed me as an intercessor and in doing so God gave me a passion to pray for others. You see as women of God and an Intercessor it was my duty to intercede for them. When my training was over God healed me of my pulmonary issues.

Personal Emergency

A personal crisis can occur when events of an extraordinary nature create extreme tension and stress within an individual which require major decisions or actions to resolve. A crisis situation can revolve a dangerous situation such as extreme weather conditions or a medical emergency or long-term illness. A crisis can also be related to a change in events that comprise the day-to-day life of a person and those in their close circle. Such situations may be loss of a job; extreme financial hardship; alcoholism or addiction and other situations that are life altering and require action that is outside the "normal" daily routine.

This can be Your Duty Intercessors in Mass Crisis

And the rain descended, and the floods came, and the winds blew, and beat upon that house; and it fell not: for it was founded upon a rock. Mat 7:25

Be that rock in emergencies. Intercessors are in a unique position to respond to individual needs in ways that no other organization or group can because you can walk in the middle of a crisis and pray quietly. No one needs to know why you are there. Crisis Intercessor can demonstrate the love of Christ as they meet the needs of victims in the time of Crisis every-day. Emergency Intercessors Community Leadership can be helpful if it is coordinated with or without the efforts of other Emergency relief agencies.

Building a relationship with crisis relief agencies and services are a variety of ways you can be useful. The Network relationship can offer service and agencies for food, clothing, and counseling and assistance for special needs. Additional opportunities for agencies and services in an Emergency can be used as a distribution center for clothing or bulk food items, an information staging area for volunteers or work units; a shelter, a childcare center, a communication center, or an information center for other organizations. Pray for them they need your prayers.

Training your community network can provide a ready pool of volunteers to perform any of the above services. They can also provide transportation and assist with cleanup and repair. Crisis agencies can provide counseling and assistance for special needs.

The churches within community could be a gathering point for food, supplies, building materials, and other items contributed by the community. It could be used as an orientation center for untrained people who have volunteered to help in the Crisis area, a shelter for volunteers from outside the area, a staging area for mobile unit's en-route to the Crisis site, a communications center, or a command center. There should be Intercessors praying for this to be taking place and for those that are in charge. Standing in the gape that everything will be done in order.

American Red Cross and The Salvation Army – In most disaster situations these organizations are on the scene. Red Cross helps with sheltering prior to a storm.

Red Cross Shelters operation training is required for all Crisis Intercessors or Chaplains and must communicate with the Red Cross and receive all Crisis (disaster training) that the Red Cross offers. Also, Red Cross provides help with food distribution after a storm. There training want cost you anything.

The Salvation Army also helps with feeding after a storm as well as long-term recovery help. Both of these organizations can offer crucial help after a storm to help communities recover.

Emergency management (or **disaster management**) is the discipline of dealing with and avoiding risks. It is a discipline that involves preparing for disaster before it occurs, disaster response.

Emergency management (or **disaster management**) is the discipline of dealing with and avoiding risks. It is a discipline that involves preparing for disaster before it occurs. Train with them and learn what to do if a disaster hit your community. Be prepared, be ready have your team in place know what to do.

Chapter 6

Politics and Intercessors

If there were ever a time in the American history that we should line up with the word of God it is now. We should be praying these scriptures every day for the people that are working in our government. When the illegitimate white supremacist President Trump was put in office the night of the election God gave me a vision I saw a serpent with two (2) rings around his neck with Donald Trump face on the head of the serpent. The interpretation of the rings around Donald Trump neck represent Russia and power or privilege.

The Prophet's Dictionary "says it is a snake, creepers and a creature that from antiquity and is believed to symbolize magic powers, mysterious knowledge, fertility, and power of darkness". With Donald Trump in office an open prophetic allusion to the United States, a nation founded by those once held under the oppressions of both religious and personal persecution, who through its Constitution vowed to uphold religious tolerance and the free will of all men through republicanism (government by the people, for the people). This once strong and powerful blessed nation of God that was the hallmark of Protestantism world-wide cannot surrender its allegiance to his creature Donald Trump and his ideas. It will open up doors and strongholds you want be able to close. The message and time in prophecy is given by the term "hour", such as: "For the Holy Spirit shall teach you in the same hour what you ought to say" Luke 12:12 – marking the wise who are sealed and empowered by the Holy Spirit to give their testimony on behalf of the Truth "To us, as God's servants, has been entrusted the third angel's message, the binding-off message, that is to prepare a people for the coming of our King." Prepare for war.

It is in my opinion illegitimate white supremacist President Trump has perform the scripture John 10:10 The thief cometh not, but for to steal, and to kill, and to destroy: And this is why we should be praying these scriptures with the understanding as God's servants the worker should go to work with the whole of God every day.

Servants, be obedient to them that are your masters according to the flesh, with fear and trembling, in singleness of your heart, as unto Christ; Not with eyeservice, as men pleasers; but as the servants of Christ, doing the will of God from the heart; With good will doing service, as to the Lord, and not to men: Knowing that whatsoever good thing any man doeth, the same shall he receive of the Lord, whether he be bond or free. And, you master, do the same things unto them, forbearing threatening: knowing that your Master also is in heaven; neither is there respect of persons with him.

When I was in politics I never left my home without being prayed up. My prayer partner of twenty years Sister Zarlee Dillion prayed a prayer of agreement with me for every event and meetings I attended. I was always covered by prayer. Prayer helped me to maneuver in the mist of all the people that let the devil use them. And these people were evil with a smile.

We would always pray this prayer that if any one mint me any harm we would bind them from my presents and only people that wish good things for me would be release to inter into my present. We would bind evil and loose good. We took God at his word: And I will give unto thee the keys of the kingdom of heaven: and whatsoever thou shalt bind on earth shall be bound in heaven: and whatsoever thou shalt loose on earth shall be loosed in heaven. Matthew 16:19 We also prayed that I would walk in love and be received in love and that whatever I would speak would be spoken out of love. Whatever I was going to do for God it was to be done out of Love.

God has given us power over our enemies when we learn how to kill our flesh and walk in His Spirit. God wants us to embrace His Grace and the principles of His word, and to love Him with our whole hearts. It is the mandate that our light shine so that the world can see that we are not of the world; but that we are the ones that belongs to God. I took a position that not to do business with corrupt leaders and all of the years of humiliation I endured, were not in vain. In the year 2004 I made Businesswoman of the year.

We should be an influence to others by the way we walk in Christ; loving one another with the understanding that the things that we do for Christ will last. Praying for one another in the good times and the bad times. Speaking good and not evil toward one another. Knowing that it starts with me when I ask God the question, am I the one with the problem?

The Whole Armor of God

Finally, my brethren, be strong in the Lord, and in the power of his might. Put on the whole armor of God, that you may be able to stand against the wiles of the devil. For we wrestle not against flesh and blood, but against principalities, against powers, against the rulers of the darkness of this world and against the spiritual wickedness in high places. Wherefore take unto you the whole armor of God, that you may be able to withstand in the evil day, and having done all, to stand. I was praying for the whole armor of God because the Spirit let me know I would need it. One-night while I was sleeping the Holy Spirit came on me and spiritual place each piece of the armor of God on me.

Stand therefore, having your loins girt about with truth, and having on the breastplate of righteousness; And your feet shod with the preparation of the gospel of peace; Above all, taking the shield of faith, wherewith you shall be able to quench all the fiery darts of the wicked. And take the helmet of salvation, and the sword of the Spirit, which is the word of God: Praying always with all prayer and supplication in the Spirit and watching thereunto with all perseverance and supplication for all saints; I prayed every day not to walk in my righteousness but to walk in God righteousness.

God help me to stand with the gospel of peace in prayer strengthening me in faith and his word and giving me an over flow of His Spirit every time I went into the political arena. Sometimes my anointing was like fire I really had to be strong and prayed up or I would not have been able to stand. And for me, utterance was being given unto me, that I open my mouth boldly, to make known the mystery of the gospel, for which I am an ambassador in bonds: that therein I may speak boldly, as I ought to speak. Grace be with all of you that love our Lord Jesus Christ in sincerity.

What You Need to Know

The Republican Party is one of the two major contemporary political parties in the United States, along with the Democratic Party. It is often called the Grand Old Party or the GOP. Founded in Ripon, Wisconsin, in 1854 by anti-slavery expansion activists and modernizers, the Republican Party quickly surpassed the Whig Party as the principal opposition to the Democratic Party.

It first came to power in 1860 with the election of Abraham Lincoln to the presidency and presided over the American Civil War and Reconstruction. Today, the party flipped and support everything that is against the American people. They are not a conservative and/or center-right platform any longer, with further foundations that is for the 1% and no longer follow the constitution policies of the United State.

The Republican Party is currently the second largest party with 55 million registered voters as of 2004, encompassing roughly one-third of the electorate. Republicans currently fill a minority of seats in both the United States Senate and the House of Representatives, hold a minority of state governorships, and control a minority of state legislatures with an illegitimate white supremacist President

The Democratic Party is one of the two major contemporary political parties in the United States, along with the Republican Party. It is the oldest political party in continuous operation in the United States and it is one of the oldest parties in the world. Today, the party supports a liberal and/or center-left platform.

The Democratic Party traces its origins to the Democratic-Republican Party, founded by Thomas Jefferson, James Madison, and other influential opponents of the Federalists in 1792. However, the modern Democratic party truly arose in the 1830s, with the election of Andrew Jackson.

Since the division of the Republican Party in the election of 1912, it has gradually positioned itself to the left of the Republican Party on economic and social issues. Until the period following the passage of the Civil Rights Act of 1964, the Democratic Party was primarily a coalition of two parties divided by region. Southern Democrats were typically given high conservative ratings by the American Conservative Union while northern Democrats were typically given very low ratings. Southern Democrats were a core bloc of the bipartisan conservative coalition that lasted through the Reagan-era.

The economically activist philosophy of Franklin D. Roosevelt, which has strongly influenced American liberalism, has shaped much of the party's economic agenda since 1932, and served to tie the two regional factions of the party together until the late 1960s. In fact, Roosevelt's New Deal coalition usually controlled the national government until the 1970s.

In politics, an **independent** or non-**party** politician is an individual NOT affiliated to any political party. Independents may hold a centrist viewpoint between those of major political parties, or they may have a viewpoint based on issues that they do not feel that any major party addresses.

Although most people believe that the United States has ONLY TWO political parties... We actually have more than seven major political parties now. The two most popular parties, Republicans and Democrats, are often referred to as "the lesser of two evils" by both sides.

Additional political parties, most often referred to as 3rd-party candidates, include: the TEA Party, the Constitution Party, the Libertarian Party, the Green Party, the Independent Party, and the Independence Party. Candidates running without a political endorsement from any party are known as Independent Candidates.

"We have a One Big Government Party system. It has a Republican wing that likes war and deficits and assaults on civil liberties and a Democratic wing that likes welfare and taxes and attacks on commercial liberties. It doesn't care about your freedoms because in exercising them you are an obstacle to its power. And it will do anything to stay in power." This can be your group to guide spiritual to do the will of God. This is ministry.

— Judge Andrew Napolitano

"The League of Women Voters is withdrawing sponsorship of the presidential debates ... because the demands of the two campaign organizations would perpetrate a fraud on the American voter. It has become clear to us that the candidates' organizations aim to add debates to their list of campaign-trail charades devoid of substance, spontaneity and answers to tough questions. The League has no intention of becoming an accessory to the hoodwinking of the American public." Pray for the League of women at election time. Join this group so you can be in the Know, be that intercessor to spiritual guide them to do it God's way.

— League of Women Voters on October 2, 1988

It All comes Down to Politics

Politics : is the process and method of gaining or maintaining support for public or common action: the conduct of decision-making for groups. This notion predates human society. Although it is most usually applied to governments, political behavior is also observed in corporate, academic, religious, and other institutions.

Political science is the field devoted to studying political behavior and examining the acquisition and application of power, or the ability to impose one's will on another. Its practitioners are known as political scientists. Political scientists look at elections, public opinion, institutional activities (how legislatures act, the relative importance of various sources of political power), the ideologies behind various politicians and interest groups, how politicians achieve and wield their influence, and so on.

Prayer is like political behavior and examining the acquisition and application of power, or the ability for God to impose his will on another. Political behavior needs Go to impose his will because absolute power corrupt.

When a nation departs from the ways of God, from faith, the nation is wide open for the devil to lead the nation astray with his seducing spirits in political behavior. It is the devil business to sell everyone a brand of corrupt political behavior to do his on biding. Satan will not allow you to take his specified place unless these powers are put into action and I mean Spiritual Warfare. We must not wait upon the enemy engage to us in combat, but we should engage the enemy before he starts. In spiritual warfare we can bind the evil and loose the good.

I served twelve years as an intercessor in the political arena and the first thing I learned was never to go in that arena without prayer and I mean prayer with your spiritual language, because the demonic spirits will meet you at the door and you will need to be prayed up to make it through that day's journey taking authority before your journey began.

All disobedient spirits are subject to us through God. Why should this nation of people neglect this great tool of BINDING POWER"? This power will aid us to win and to keep, and to nourish the Political behavior of our nation and those who God has call to serve the people of this nation, an army of Intercessors interceding in all areas of our nation political arena.

Federal Government
State Government
City Government
Election
Precinct Chairman or Caption
Polling Places
Early Voting and
Election Day

You can sever as an Intercessor for any Federal Government, State Government, and City Government on Boards and committees pray for your federal, city and state officials. These people make decisions that will affect us all. Your prayers can spiritually help them make the right decision. And we can truly be the nation under God.

Government Election

There has never been a time when our government has been openly operating in so much demon spirits than today. This government need intercessors pulling down stronghold to deliver this government and nation from the demonic forces that are governing this nation at this time. Prayer can change this nation and government. This battle that our nation and government are fighting today is not a battle for the flesh it is a spiritual battle. The bible teaches us about this battle that we find our self in, in the book of (Ephesians 6:12).

For we wrestle not against flesh and blood, but against principalities, against powers, against the rulers of the darkness of this world, against spiritual wickedness in high places.

Spiritual filled Intercessor that operate in the gift of intercession have equipped themselves for the battle. They have put the whole armor of God, that they may be able to stand against the tricks of the devil. I remember when God equipped me with the whole armor of God. I had been praying for the armor of God and one night about three o'clock in the morning the Holy Spirit came into my room and equipped me, it was a Spiritual journey in the spiritual ream that I will never forget I had received Spiritually every piece of the armor.

As an Intercessor in the political arena I needed the whole armor of God. Let's take time out and look at our government process and what areas you can service as an intercessor. Why? Because the Bible says Every place where-on the soles of your feet shall tread shall be yours: from the wilderness and Lebanon, from the river, the river

Euphrates, even unto the uttermost sea shall your coast be. (Deuteronomy 11:24)

How to Possess Land

Spiritual filled Intercessor or intercessor or if you can pray or read the Bible can possess the land. You can operate in the gift of intercession or stand on God's word have equipped themselves for the battle. You can and will possess the land, because God hear your prayers and He answer them.

Every place where-on the soles of your feet shall tread shall be yours:

Let's Take the United States

Under the United States Constitution, states may not restrict voting rights in ways that infringe one's right to equal protection under the law (Fourteenth Amendment), on the basis of race (Fifteenth Amendment), sex (Nineteenth Amendment), or age for persons age 18 and older (Twenty-Sixth Amendment).

While the federal government has jurisdiction over federal elections, most election laws are decided at the state level and the true authority to interpret and enforce those laws comes at the local level. Because of this, the administration of elections can vary widely across jurisdictions. Registering to vote is the responsibility of individuals in the United States. Voters are not automatically registered to vote once they reach the age of 18. Every state except North Dakota requires that citizens who wish to vote be registered.

Traditionally, voters had to register at state offices to vote, but in the mid-1990s efforts were made by the federal government to make registering easier, in an attempt to increase turnout. The National Voter Registration Act of 1993 (the "Motor Voter" law) forced state governments to make the voter registration process easier by providing uniform registration services through drivers' license registration centers, disability centers, schools, libraries, and mail-in registration. Some states allow citizens to register to vote on the same day of the election, known as Election Day Registration. States with same-day registration are exempt from Motor Voter, namely: Idaho, Minnesota, New Hampshire, North Dakota, Wisconsin, and Wyoming.

Voters may register at the local election office (which is usually at city or town hall) or, one may call the election department and request a voter registration form through the mail. Voter registration forms may be found at public libraries and registries of motor vehicles. These forms must be filled out and mailed to the local election department. Also, one may register at a voter registration drive. The only states with online voter registration are Arizona and Washington, though legislation has been introduced in other states.

Some states prohibit individuals convicted of a felony from voting, known as felony disenfranchisement. One may register wherever one has an address, regardless of its permanence—for example, a college student living away from home may register to vote in the college's city, even if that is not a permanent address. In most states, one must register, usually 30 days before a given election, in order to vote in it. Seven states, Idaho, Iowa, Maine, Minnesota, New Hampshire, Wisconsin and Wyoming, allow for Election Day Registration.

In some states, when registering to vote, one may declare an affiliation with a political party. This declaration of affiliation does not cost any money, and it is not the same as being a dues-paying member of a party; for example, a party cannot prevent anybody from declaring his or her affiliation with them, but it can refuse requests for full membership. Some states, including Michigan, Virginia, and Washington do not have party affiliation with registration.

In general elections, a voter may choose to vote for all of a particular party's candidates (**straight-ticket voting**) or to vote for candidates from different parties for different offices (Party X's candidate for President, Party Y's candidate for Senator, Party Z's candidate for Governor). In a general election, one's political party affiliation does not determine which party's candidates one may vote for.

Election Day Registration

In the United States, Election Day Registration, also known as "same-day voter registration," permits eligible citizens to register and vote on Election Day. Election Day Registration significantly increases the opportunity for all citizens to cast a vote and participate in democracy.

Nine states have some form of Election Day Registration: Idaho, Iowa, Maine, Minnesota, Montana, New Hampshire, North Carolina, Wisconsin and Wyoming.

(<u>Montana</u> enacted the practice for the first time in 2006. <u>North Carolina</u> first implemented their plan in the fall of 2007. And <u>Iowa</u> began EDR in 2008). (<u>Connecticut</u> also has EDR, but only for casting votes for the Presidency. It should also be noted that <u>North Dakota</u> has no voter registration requirement at all.) Under the new system in place in North Carolina, same-day registration occurs three to nineteen days before the scheduled election.

Early Voting

Early voting is the process by which voters can cast their vote on a single or series of days prior to an election. Early voting can take place remotely, such as by mail, or in person, usually in designated early voting <u>polling stations</u>. The availability and time periods for early voting vary based on jurisdiction and type of election. The goal of early voting is usually to increase participation and relieve congestion of <u>polling stations</u> on <u>Election Day</u>.

An advance poll (also "advance voting") is held in some <u>elections</u> to allow participation by voters who may not be able to <u>vote</u> on the set election day(s). This may include people who will be out of the polling area during the election period, <u>poll</u> workers, <u>campaign</u> workers, people with medical procedures scheduled for that time, among others

Polling Place

A polling place or polling station (the latter is the less common usage, but favored in the <u>United Kingdom</u> and standard in Canada) is where <u>voters</u> cast their <u>ballots</u> in <u>elections</u>.

Since elections generally take place over a one- or two-day span on a periodic basis, often annual or longer, polling places are often located in facilities used for other purposes, such as <u>schools</u>, <u>sports halls</u>, local government <u>offices</u>, or even private homes, and will each serve a similar number of people. The area may be known as a <u>ward</u>, <u>precinct</u>, <u>polling district</u> or <u>constituency</u>.

The polling place is staffed with officials (who may be called <u>election judges</u>, <u>returning officers</u> or other titles) who monitor the voting procedures and assist voters with the election process. Scrutineer (or poll-watchers) are independent or partisan observers who attend the poll to ensure the impartiality of the process.

The facility will be open between specified hours depending upon the type of election, and political activity by or on behalf of those standing in the ballot is usually prohibited within the venue and immediately surrounding area.

Inside the polling place wills be an area (usually a <u>voting booth</u>) where the voter may select the candidate or party of their choice in secret, and if a ballot paper is used this will be placed into a <u>ballot box</u> in front of witnesses but who cannot see the actual selection made. <u>Voting machines</u> may be employed instead. Some polling places are temporary structures. A portable cabin may be specially sited for an election and removed afterwards.

Precinct

A **precinct** is a space enclosed by the walls or other boundaries of a particular place or building, or by an arbitrary and imaginary line drawn around it. The term has several different uses. It can, for example, refer to a division of a police department in a large city.

Precinct chairman or captain

A precinct/chairman or captain is the individual who acts as the direct link between a political party organization (which sometimes acts as a party machine) and the voters in an election precinct. A precinct captain helps with voter registration, distribution of literature and other promotional efforts, and helps voters get absentee ballots or get to the voting booths on Election Day.

Elections

A precinct is generally the lowest-level minor civil division in the United States and in that context is also known in some places as an **election district**. Precincts usually do not have separate governmental authorities, but for purposes of conducting elections, a minor civil division such as a county or township is typically subdivided into precincts and each address is assigned to a specific precinct.

Each precinct has a specific location where its residents go to vote. Sometimes several precincts will use the same polling station. A 2004 survey by the United States Election Assistance Commission reported an average precinct size in the United States of approximately 1,100 registered voters. Kansas had the smallest average precinct size with 437 voters per precinct, while the District of Columbia had the largest average size at 2,704 voters per precinct.

Political parties often designate individuals, known by various titles such as "precinct captain" or "Precinct Committee Officer," to help them keep track of how the voters in a precinct feel about candidates and issues, and to encourage people to vote.

Precinct data are not widely available, though they can often be obtained by request. The Canadian equivalent of a precinct is known as a Poll.

Election Day Registration

In the United States, Election Day Registration, also known as "same-day voter registration," permits eligible citizens to register and vote on Election Day. Election Day Registration significantly increases the opportunity for all citizens to cast a vote and participate in democracy.

Nine states have some form of Election Day Registration: Idaho, Iowa, Maine, Minnesota, Montana, New Hampshire, North Carolina, Wisconsin and Wyoming. (Montana enacted the practice for the first time in 2006. North Carolina first implemented their plan in the fall of 2007. And Iowa began EDR in 2008). (Connecticut also has EDR, but only for casting votes for the Presidency. It should also be noted that North Dakota has no voter registration requirement at all.) Under the new system in place in North

Carolina, same-day registration occurs three to nineteen days before the scheduled election.

Early voting

Early voting is the process by which voters can cast their vote on a single or series of days prior to an election. Early voting can take place remotely, such as by mail, or in person, usually in designated early voting polling stations. The availability and time periods for early voting vary based on jurisdiction and type of election. The goal of early voting is usually to increase participation and relieve congestion of polling stations on Election Day.

An advance poll (also "advance voting") is held in some elections to allow participation by voters who may not be able to vote on the set election day(s). This may include people who will be out of the polling area during the election period, poll workers, campaign workers, people with medical procedures scheduled for that time, among others.

Polling place

A polling place or polling station (the latter is the less common usage, but favored in the United Kingdom and standard in Canada)[1][2] is where voters cast their ballots in elections.

Since elections generally take place over a one- or two-day span on a periodic basis, often annual or longer, polling places are often located in facilities used for other purposes, such as schools, sports halls, local government offices, or even private homes, and will each serve a similar number of people. The area may be known as a ward, precinct, polling district or constituency. The polling place is staffed with officials (who may be called election judges, returning officers or other titles) who monitor the voting procedures and assist voters with the election process. Scrutineer (or poll-watchers) are independent or partisan observers who attend the poll to ensure the impartiality of the process.

The facility will be open between specified hours depending upon the type of election, and political activity by or on behalf of those standing in the ballot is usually prohibited within the venue and immediately surrounding area. Inside the polling place wills be an area (usually a voting booth) where the voter may select the candidate or party of their choice in secret, and if a ballot paper is used this will be placed into a ballot box in front of witnesses but who cannot see the actual selection made. Voting machines may be employed instead.

Some polling places are temporary structures. A portable cabin may be specially sited for an election and removed afterwards.

Precinct

A **precinct** is a space enclosed by the walls or other boundaries of a particular place or building, or by an arbitrary and imaginary line drawn around it. The term has several different uses. It can, for example, refer to a division of a police department in a large city. A good place for prayer walks or as a intercessor quietly praying through the day.

Precinct chairman or captain

A precinct/chairman or captain is the individual who acts as the direct link between a <u>political party organization</u> (which sometimes acts as a <u>party machine</u>) and the voters in an election <u>precinct</u>. A precinct captain helps with voter registration, distribution of literature and other promotional efforts, and helps voters get <u>absentee ballots</u> or get to the voting booths on Election Day.

Elections

A precinct is generally the lowest-level <u>minor civil division</u> in the <u>United States</u> and in that context is also known in some places as an **election district**. Precincts usually do not have separate governmental authorities, but for purposes of conducting elections, a minor civil division such as a <u>county</u> or <u>township</u> is typically subdivided into precincts and each address is assigned to a specific precinct.

Each precinct has a specific location where its residents go to vote. Sometimes several precincts will use the same <u>polling station</u>. A 2004 survey by the United States <u>Election Assistance Commission</u> reported an average precinct size in the United States of approximately 1,100 registered voters. <u>Kansas</u> had the smallest average precinct size with 437 voters per precinct, while the <u>District of Columbia</u> had the largest average size at 2,704 voters per precinct.

Political parties often designate individuals, known by various titles such as "precinct captain" or "Precinct Committee Officer," to help them keep track of how the voters in a precinct feel about candidates and issues, and to encourage people to vote.

Precinct data are not widely available, though they can often be obtained by request. The Canadian equivalent of a precinct is known as a Poll. A Precinct Chairman or Captain are delegate in the City, State and National Convention. I served in all of the

In the political arena I served or participated in the above positions. I to had learned how to press my way through the fire, the storms the trials and everything that came my way to destroy me. I stayed close to God and God alone gets all the glory. I could not have made it without God. Because I know that I can do nothing without God, and I am nothing without God for God is my provider.

God also is my source and my resources. I know that I am equipped for the battles that will come, and they will come, but I also know that with God as my head, He will give me victory over every battle if I stay close to Him! I have a good understanding, it is not about me, because it is all about Him.

I received a letter inviting me to attend a meeting from one of the Senators from out of Houston. I went to the meeting, and in that meeting was a room full of people that had the character of alley cats. The Senator wanted me to form a corporation with these people. I don't want to judge them, but I knew that they had come to steal, kill, and to destroy me. When I walked out of that meeting, I said to the Lord; I refuse to do business with anyone in that room, because I will not do business with people I cannot turn by back on. I was pro-life and they were pro-choice.

I said to the Lord; "if my name was going to be use, the corporation would be run with integrity or I would not have anything to do with it. Because I rejected them, they made my political journey a living hell. I took that position not to do business with corrupt leaders and I endured years of humiliation, rejection and disappointments. Today I am grateful for them because it helped make me the woman of God that I am today. I had learned how to press my way through the fire, the storms the trials and everything that came my way to destroy me. Now I can say to all of Thank You for the journey.

Chapter 7

The Call of an Intercessor

As an Intercessor, you have been given the greatest privilege and responsibility in all the world: called to be an Intercessor of the living God, called by the sovereign Lord and Majesty of the universe. Chosen by God Himself and chosen by His Son Jesus Christ and by the Holy Spirit of God. You have been called to be an Intercessor by the gift of God grace. You are an ambassador for Christ, and you are counted trustworthy and faithful by Christ.

You must always pray the word and you should labor in prayer and in prayer you must seek the lost and pray for their salvation and pray that God will send labors for the harvest. As an intercessor it is for you to teach and equip this generation for the next generation of intercessor. In the spiritual ream you are the one that have authority as the overseer of good and evil in the church standing in the gap for your leaders and the watchman that watch over the believers in the spiritual ream.

<u>What your resources are as an intercessor:</u> You can fulfill the purposes of God in your life and ministry as an intercessor, because you are not alone you don't just have human wisdom and strength to accomplish your task in God. He has provided you with great help-unbelievable resources to equip you to live for him and to carry out His great purposes for you.

- ❖ You have the grace and power of Christ.
- ❖ You have been given the presence and power of the Holy Spirit.
- ❖ You are given the presence and Power of God the Father.
- ❖ You are given the assurance absolute assurance of victory by God Himself.
- ❖ You are given Spiritual Gift by God.
- ❖ You have been given faith to sustain you as an Intercessor.
- ❖ You have the Love of Christ to compel you as an Intercessor.
- ❖ And you are given hope of the resurrection to sustain you and your ministry.

There are three essential things that are absolute in your ministry as an intercessor, in this broken world. It must always be you and Christ Jesus and the word of God must be your map to deliverance, healing, correction, praise, knowledge with understanding and wisdom and prayer should always be your only means for direction. It is your responsibility to make sure that your belief in Christ is the right kind of belief so study Christ and get to know Him for yourself and make sure that you are a new creation in Christ Jesus.

Intercessors live by the word of God and proclaim it and with the help of the Holy Spirit we can change into the image of Christ by lining up our lives with the word of God and constantly examining our self so we can be renewed daily always seeking first the kingdom of God and all His Righteousness. When we pray we should always start our prayer as Christ taught us to pray with the Lord's prayer that covers all of our needs because it is the divine order of prayer.

Your Desires in Christ

Your main desire in Christ should be to walk in love because God is Love. Love covers or remove all of our dislike, mean felling we have toward each other and deliver us from the spirits of hate, deception, control and manipulation. And all that you will do for Christ, will be done out of love. This is one of yours keys to the kingdom of God, is to know that everything about God is love, so desire to walk in it. It will teach you to consider or be mindful of other and not always only thinking of yourself. Intercessors always pray for others.

You should become so faithful that you are totally surrendered to Christ to the end of your walk. You must know, believe and understand God. Because the Lord said "Bring forth the blind people that have eyes, and the deaf that have ears. Let all the nations be gathered together, and let the people be assembled: who among them can declare this, and shew us former things? let them bring forth their witnesses, that they may be justified: or let them hear, and say, It is truth.

You are my witnesses, saith the LORD, and my servant whom I have chosen: that you may know and believe me, and understand that I am he: before me there was no God formed, neither shall there be after me. I, even I, am the LORD; and beside me there is no savior. I have declared, and have saved, and I have shewed, when there was no strange god among you: therefore you are my witnesses, saith the LORD, that I am God." Isaiah 43:8-12

This is the reason God created you, saved you and called into the ministry of Intercession or as an Intercessor that you may know Him, believe Him and understand Him. Your desire must be to be conformed to Christ's death and to totally subject yourself to God and deny yourself and put your fleshly desires to death and to do the will of God. You must forget the pass and press on for the prize. I leave you with this, not as though I had already attained, either were already perfect: but I follow after, if that I may apprehend that for which also I am apprehended of Christ Jesus.

Brethren, I count not myself to have apprehended: but this one thing I do, forgetting those things which are behind, and reaching forth unto those things which are before, I press toward the mark for the prize of the high calling of God in Christ Jesus. Philippians 3:12-14

The apostle was constant in prayer, that the believers might be filled with the knowledge of God's will, in all wisdom. God words will not do without good works. He, who undertakes to give strength to his people, is a God of power, and of glorious power. The blessed Spirit is the author of this. In praying for spiritual strength, we are not straitened, or confined in the promises, and should not be so in our hopes and desires. The grace of God in the hearts of believers is the power of God; and there is glory in this power.

The special use of this strength was for sufferings. There is work to be done, even when we are suffering. Amidst all their trials they gave thanks to the Father of our Lord Jesus, whose special grace fitted them to partake of the inheritance provided for the saints. To bring about this change, those were made willing subjects of Christ, who were slaves of Satan. All who are designed for heaven hereafter are prepared for heaven now. Those who have the inheritance of sons, have the education of sons, and the disposition of sons. By faith in Christ they enjoyed this redemption, as the purchase of his atoning blood, whereby forgiveness of sins and all other spiritual blessings were bestowed. Surely then we shall deem it a favor to be delivered from Satan's kingdom and brought into that of Christ, knowing that all trials will soon end, and that every believer will be found among those who come out of great tribulation.

Knowledge is given to the intercessors to open spiritual things in scriptures, of revelation knowledge to be revealed by His Anointed to His people. The scribes and lawyers held this key with jealous care. They reserved them exclusively to themselves. Our Lord likened the key of knowledge unto a temple into which the lawyers, writers, and leaders should have led the people into, but instead they refused to enter in or let the people in with their keys. They not only hindered the people from knowing but even nullified God's commands with their traditional doctrine. So...Jesus told them off, pronounced a woe on them...took the key of knowledge away from them. I would say that some are in that position today. You have keys, so don't let it be you the one that hinders others. God will give the key to divine strategies to intercede on behalf of others when you ask God. I close with this in mind:

They shall not labor in vain, nor bring forth for trouble; for they are the seed of the blessed of the LORD, and their offspring with them. And it shall come to pass, that before they call, I will answer; and while they are yet speaking, I will hear. Isaiah 65:23-24

Dr. Emma T. Warren, Chaplain

Dr. Warren the publish Author, Chaplain and God's Prophetess dedicated Intercessor is respected as a woman of prayer throughout her family, friends and ministry associates and she is forever grateful to God for the journey of teaching her excellence in the Ministry of Prayer. Her Love for God has granted her wisdom and prudence; the comforts of his presence, the comforts of his Love, the influence of his Spirit, the and the enjoyment of his Ministry. I am forever grateful for this journey and walk with God.

Dr. Warren Prayer for You

Our Father which art in heaven, Holy is your name. Your kingdom come your will be done on earth, as it is in heaven. I thank you God through Jesus Christ for you all, that their faith is spoken of throughout the whole world. For you God are my witness, whom I serve with my spirit and whole heart in the gospel of your Son Jesus, that without ceasing I make mention of all of you always in my prayers, my prayer request if by any means at length I may have a prosperous journey by the will of God to come to you. For I long to see you, that I may impart to you some spiritual gift, to the end that you may be established.

That is, that I may be comforted together with you, by the Holy Spirit and faith both of you and me. For I am not ashamed of the gospel of Christ: for it is the power of God to salvation to everyone that believeth. For in this is the righteousness of God revealed from faith to faith: as it is written, the just shall live by faith. Even so then at this present time may we be the remnant according to the election of grace.

Now may the God of hope fill you with all joy and peace in believing, that you may abound in hope, through the power of the Holy Spirit and that God's Grace will over power you in all that you do and grant you wisdom, knowledge, revelation and most of all understand of Him and who God truly is.

Dr. Emma T. Warren, Chaplain

BIBLIOGRAPHY

Note Chapter Seven (7): The information in this chapter was compiled by Chaplain (General) Phillip D. Burnette, National Commander, and United States Corps of Chaplains, is a combination of various statements from all over the web and as such constitutes a work that could be considered as in the public domain.

The King James Bible

From Wikipedia, the free encyclopedia: Political Parties

The United States presidential elections use an electoral college to determine the winner and the electors are chosen by popular vote in each state. Voters choose a slate of electors that are supporting one of the candidates, although this may not be obvious to the voter at the time.

Registered Democrats, Republicans and independents in millions as of 2004. Third party membership is too small to show; in millions, major third party memberships are: Constitution Party, .37; Green Party, .31; Libertarian Party, .2 [1]

The modern political party system in the United States is a two-party system dominated by the Democratic Party and the Republican Party. These two parties have won every United States presidential election since 1852 and have controlled the United States Congress since at least 1856.

Several other third parties from time to time achieve relatively minor representation at the national and state levels.

The **Constitution Party** is a conservative United States political party. It was founded as the **U.S. Taxpayers Party** in 1992. The party's official name was changed to the *Constitution Party* in 1999; however, some state affiliate parties are known under different names.

According to ballot access expert Richard Winger, the editor of *Ballot Access News*, who periodically compiles and analyzes voter registration statistics as reported by state voter agencies, it ranks third nationally amongst all United States political parties in registered voters, with 366,937 registered members as of November 2006.

The Constitution Party advocates a platform that purports to reflect the Founding Fathers' original intent of the U.S. Constitution, principles found in the U.S. Declaration of Independence, and morals taken from the Bible.

In 2006, Rick Jore of Montana became the first Constitution Party candidate elected to a state-level office[9][10], though the Constitution Party of Montana had disaffiliated itself from the national party a short time before the election.

The Constitution Party's 2008 presidential nominee was Chuck Baldwin.

SPIRITUAL SUGGESTED READING AND DVD

LIST

David Barton
Wall Builders
PO Box 397
Aledo, TX 76008
1-800-873-2845

Books

Holiness, Truth and the Presence of God
Francis Frangipane

Arrow Publications
PO Box 10102
Cedar Rapids, IA 52410
319-395-7833

Love the Way to Victory
Kenneth E. Hagin
Kenneth Hagin Ministries
PO Box 50126
Tulsa, OK 74150-0126

The Power of Agreement
Pastor Rick Hawkins
PO Box 28402
San Antonio, TX 78228
210-432-5775

Scripture Keys for Kingdom Living
June Newman
Scripture Keys Ministries
PO Box 6559
Denver, Colorado 80206-0559

DRETWC

Dr. Emma T. Warren, Chaplain

Purchase Order

SHIP TO:

Please Print:

Your Name:_____

Address: _____

Email: _____

Purchase Order #:
Date:
Vendor ID:

QUANTITY	DESCRIPTION		UNIT PRICE	TOTAL
	THE JOURNEY of an INTERCESSOR		$15.00	$15.00
			Subtotal	
			Your Tax	
Mail To:			Shipping	$4.00
			Balance Due	

Dr. Emma T. Warren
2260 Ferdon Blvd Suite 110
Crestview FL 32536

Fax: To: 1-888-612-7721
Email: tw.emma@nym.hush.com

THE JOURNEY of an INTERCESSOR

ORETWC

Dr. Emma T. Warren, Chaplain

Purchase Order

SHIP TO:

Please Print:

Your Name:_____

Address: _____

Email: _____

Purchase Order #:
Date:
Vendor ID:

QUANTITY		DESCRIPTION		UNIT PRICE	TOTAL
		THE JOURNEY of an INTERCESSOR		$15.00	$15.00

		Subtotal	
		Your Tax	
Mail To:		Shipping	$4.00
		Balance Due	

Dr. Emma T. Warren
2260 Ferdon Blvd Suite 110
Crestview FL 32536

Fax: To: 1-888-612-7721
Email: tw.emma@nym.hush.com

THE JOURNEY of an INTERCESSOR

THE JOURNEY of an INTERCESSOR

ORETWC

Dr. Emma T. Warren, Chaplain

Purchase Order

SHIP TO:

Please Print:

Your Name:_____

Address: _____

Email:_____

Purchase Order #:
Date:
Vendor ID:

QUANTITY		DESCRIPTION		UNIT PRICE	TOTAL
		THE JOURNEY of an INTERCESSOR		$15.00	$15.00

	Subtotal	
	Your Tax	
Mail To:	Shipping	$4.00
	Balance Due	

Dr. Emma T. Warren
2260 Ferdon Blvd Suite 110
Crestview FL 32536

Fax: To: 1-888-612-7721
Email: tw.emma@nym.hush.com

THE JOURNEY of an INTERCESSOR

DRETWC

Dr. Emma T. Warren, Chaplain

Purchase Order

SHIP TO:

Please Print:

Your Name:_____

Address: _____

Email:_____

Purchase Order #:
Date:
Vendor ID:

QUANTITY	DESCRIPTION	UNIT PRICE	TOTAL
	THE JOURNEY of an INTERCESSOR	$15.00	$15.00
		Subtotal	
		Your Tax	
		Shipping	$4.00
		Balance Due	

Mail To:

Dr. Emma T. Warren
2260 Ferdon Blvd Suite 110
Crestview FL 32536

Fax: To: 1-888-612-7721
Email: tw.emma@nym.hush.com

NOTES

THE JOURNEY of an INTERCESSOR

DRETWC

Dr. Emma T. Warren, Chaplain

Purchase Order

SHIP TO:

Please Print:

Your Name: _____

Address: _____

Email: _____

Purchase Order #:
Date:
Vendor ID:

QUANTITY	DESCRIPTION		UNIT PRICE	TOTAL
	THE JOURNEY of an INTERCESSOR		$15.00	$15.00
			Subtotal	
			Your Tax	
Mail To:			Shipping	$4.00
Dr. Emma T. Warren			Balance Due	

Dr. Emma T. Warren
2260 Ferdon Blvd Suite 110
Crestview FL 32536

Fax: To: 1-888-612-7721
Email: tw.emma@nym.hush.com

Page 153

NOTES

NOTES

-END-

www.ingramcontent.com/pod-product-compliance
Lightning Source LLC
Chambersburg PA
CBHW051840090426
42736CB00011B/1905